SAY THE BELLS

of

OLD MISSIONS

Legends of Old New Mexico Churches

by

Elizabeth Willis DeHuff

B. HERDER BOOK CO.
15 & 17 SOUTH BROADWAY, ST. LOUIS, MO.
AND
33 QUEEN SQUARE, LONDON, W. C.
1943

NIHIL OBSTAT

Sti. Ludovici, die 21. Nov., 1942

Wm. Fischer, S.T.D.

Censor Librorum

IMPRIMATUR

Sti. Ludovici, die 23. Nov., 1942

✠ *Joannes J. Glennon*

Archiepiscopus

Vail-Ballou Press, Inc., Binghamton and New York

To

the memory of His Excellency

ALBERT DAEGER

THE LATE ARCHBISHOP OF SANTA FE,
WHO SHOULD BE INCLUDED AMONG
THE CANON OF NEW MEXICO'S SAINTS,
PICTURED AS HE TRUDGED AFOOT MILE
UPON MILE THROUGH THESE DESERT WASTES
PERFORMING DEEDS OF MERCY, WITH ONLY
A CHUNK OF BREAD IN HIS POCKET.
I WAS HAPPY TO CALL HIM MY FRIEND.
AND
TO THE OTHER FRIENDS WHO HAVE TOLD
ME THESE STORIES THIS LITTLE BOOK
IS GRATEFULLY DEDICATED.

"You owe me five shillings,"
Say the bells of St. Helen's.

"When will you pay me?"
Say the bells of Old Bailey.

"When I grow rich,"
Say the bells of Shoreditch.

"When will that be?"
Say the bells of Stepney.

"I do not know,"
Says the great bell of Bow.

"Two sticks in an apple,"
Ring the bells of Whitechapel.

"Halfpence and farthings,"
Say the bells of St. Martin's.

"Kettles and pans,"
Say the bells of St. Ann's.

"Brickbats and tiles,"
Say the bells of St. Giles.

"Old shoes and slippers,"
Say the bells of St. Peter's.

"Pokers and tongs,"
Say the bells of St. John's.

MOTHER GOOSE

To Those Who Have Ears to Hear

Just as the bells in the churches of England rang out different tales to MOTHER GOOSE, so each group of bells in belfries of the old missions of New Mexico chimes forth its separate story.

When we speak of missions in the United States, we usually think of those magnificent old structures in California, built under the direction of Fray Junipero Serra, or perhaps of San Xavier del Bac in Arizona, famed for its story of hidden treasure and its unfinished belfry, or it may be of El Alamo in Texas. The oldest missions, however, are those in New Mexico, some of which were built more than 150 years before those of California. Because of their age and historic significance, legends—many of them delightful—have grown up around these old adobe churches. These stories are told by old men and women, who keep hearing the bells chiming these tales and who believe implicitly in what the bells say.

The first missions of New Mexico were built by those zealous Franciscan priests who came up with Juan de Oñate and his colonists in 1598. They were erected to help in the conversion of the Pueblo

Indians in their villages and for their use. Then, having settled this religious problem for the Indians, the Spanish conquistadors aided the priests in building churches for the conquerors themselves in their own *placitas,* or towns. To all this great area of *Nuevo Mejico* the Spaniards gave as patron saint, the patron saint of Old Mexico—Our Lady of Guadalupe, whose legend is one of the most miraculous.

Of course these tales are mere legends. And we may well suppose that the Indians do not confuse them with the doctrinal teaching of the Church. They are handed on from generation to generation as interesting "stories."

Contents

APPENDIX

Our Lady of Guadalupe

QUAUHTLATOHUA, who had been christened Juan Diego, drew his blanket closer.
He stepped from his adobe hut into the cold, crisp
plateau air of his Mexican village Tlaltelolco, on
a December morning in 1531.

The cold is like an Indian clown pinching my
nose, he thought. It runs like snow strings from my
finger tips to my back and makes me shiver like
dead leaves in the wind. But the padre says I must
go to Mass. I don't know, but perhaps there's magic
in this white man's God; so I go. But before he
set out on a run toward the Spanish town, Juan
Diego looked across the snow-clad earth and blew
a breath of welcome to the rising sun. Of this magic,
he was sure.

His path passed the foot of the arid, rock-covered
hill of Tepeyac, sprinkled with erratic cacti, now
white with the blanket of the Snow Woman.

As he neared Tepeyac, he heard a voice calling
to him: *Hijo mio!* ("My son!").

With a thud of moccasins on the frozen ground,
Juan stopped his trotting pace in consternation.

1

Looking up, his eyes were blinded by a dazzling light, which made the whole hillside resplendent with magical rainbow colors, glittering and pulsing. When he became accustomed to the shining glory, he saw the Virgin in its midst. It was she who had spoken to him.

Quickly Juan made the sign of the cross, fell upon his knees, and covered his face, for the splendor became too brilliant for him to look upon.

"My son," repeated the Virgin, "go to the Bishop at Mexico City and tell him to build upon this spot a chapel dedicated to me."

"Go to the Bishop, go to the Bishop," chanted Juan as he arose and ran all the way to the rectory of Fray Juan de Zumarraga, Bishop of Mexico City.

But when the Bishop heard Juan's message, he thought the poor shepherd was crazed from the monotony of his sheepherding. He would not even admit the Indian into his presence.

"Tell him to go back home and look after his sheep," ordered Fray Zumarraga.

Forgetting Mass, Juan slowly and thoughtfully wended his way back homeward. But when he again reached the foot of Tepeyac, the whole experience was repeated. Juan turned and ran again to the rectory. This time Fray Zumarraga was annoyed.

"Tell the foolish man," he exclaimed, "that I

cannot be bothered this way. Say to him that he must not come again unless he brings with him a token, a sign to prove to me that what he says is true. He must bring a token from the Virgin herself."

On Juan's return, the Virgin appeared a third time to him.

Falling upon his knees, Juan cried out: "Oh, Señora Madre, send me no more to the Bishop. He is angry. He does not believe that you have sent me. He says I must bring him a sign to prove that you have sent me."

"Then come again tomorrow, my son," said the Virgin, "and I will give you a symbol that will prove to the Bishop that I have sent you."

But when Juan reached home, he found that his uncle Juan Bernardino had fallen ill with the dangerous fever, which the Indians called *cocolixtle,* and which was usually fatal. Juan Diego was upset.

"Oh, my uncle! My uncle who is to me a father!" he wailed over and over again. In his grief he forgot the command of the Virgin.

He would not leave his uncle's bedside. On the second day after his return home, which was December 12, his uncle grew suddenly worse and seemed to be dying.

"He must not die without the priest," said Juan. "There may be magic in the words of the padre."

So he set out to fetch the priest to administer the sacrament of extreme unction.

When he neared the hill of Tepeyac, he suddenly remembered that he had not obeyed the command of the Virgin. Feeling ashamed, he took a longer path leading round the other side of the hill. But as he passed a fountain there, the Virgin appeared before him once more. Juan put his arm over his eyes to shut out the aching brightness.

"Go up on top of the hill, my son," said the Virgin. "There you will find the sign which you are to take to the Bishop to prove to him that I have sent you. Tell him again to build a chapel on this spot."

Juan Diego climbed the mountain. There before him was an unbelievable sight: roses were growing and blossoming in profusion over the arid hill-top in the blanket of snow. Timidly Juan put out his hand and touched one. It was real! Feverishly he began plucking them and folding them carefully in his *tilma* to protect them from the cold on his way to Mexico City.

With less fear, Juan knocked upon the gate of the rectory.

The Bishop was enraged when he learned that Juan had again come back.

"Why must my prayers be interrupted by this peon?" he exclaimed.

"But, Your Grace," said the page, "he says that he brings roses from the Virgin as a sign to you."

"Has the fellow completely lost his wits?" said the Bishop.

"I know not, Your Grace, but he hides something in his *tilma*."

"Then bring him in, and, if there is no sign, I shall send him away myself for good."

Before the real lace and gold-embroidered satin dress of the Bishop, Juan presented a sad figure. His pink cotton trousers were frayed. His red cotton shirt, hanging on the outside, was soiled from travel. His *tilma* was much worn from long usage, and his straw *huaraches* were ragged from running.

Juan dropped upon his knees before the magnificent presence. When he opened his *tilma* to take out the roses, he gasped and looked up at the Bishop with astonishment. The Bishop, too, leaned forward with an intake of breath. There upon the *tilma* was indelibly stamped the image of the Virgin exactly as she had appeared to Juan.

"Then what you have said is true," said His Grace. "This is truly a manifestation of our Lady. We shall build the chapel as she said, and call it the Chapel of Our Lady of Guadalupe."

At last he believed.

Juan was given food and sent home to tell the news.

It was only when he saw the peaked thatched roof of his humble mud house, that Juan remembered his uncle's illness. Filled with remorse, he rushed into the house. His uncle was no longer on his pallet. But before Juan could express his grief in a wail, his uncle walked into the room, well and strong.

"You are well!" cried Juan Diego. "When did you get well?"

And when the uncle told him that suddenly the fever had left him, they discovered that he had been healed at the very moment that the Virgin had shown herself to Juan Diego at the fountain. He knew and Juan Bernardino knew that the Virgin had cured him.

The Chapel of Our Lady of Guadalupe was built upon the site of the first appearance of the Virgin to Juan; a chapel which still stands at the top of a long row of steps, up which pilgrims daily crawl their way to behold, or touch, Juan Diego's *tilma* with the stamp of the Virgin upon it.

This legend of the *tilma* of Juan Diego is what the bells of all chapels ring out on December 12 and its eve, throughout both Old and New Mexico. And each eve of December 12, processions, carrying images of Our Lady of Guadalupe, their patron saint, along paths lighted by bonfires, take place in many towns of New Mexico, while Indians often dance in her honor in their pueblos.

Perhaps copies of the imprint upon Juan's *tilma* were brought to New Mexico with the first priests who came to convert the Indians. One of these priests was Fray Padilla, whose coffin miraculously rises from the grave. But since Fray Padilla, both alive and dead, touched the lives of men who made New Mexico history, one must understand the historical setting to appreciate this legend of Fray Padilla.

The Rising of the Coffin of
Fray Padilla

IN 1540, Francisco Vasquez de Coronado, Governor of the province of Culiacan on the west coast of Mexico, heard of seven cities of Cibola, far to the northeast. These great Indian villages were purported to be rich with gold, silver, and other treasure, according to Indian traders. So Coronado, as Francisco Vasquez is commonly called, sent messages to Spain and persuaded Charles V to equip a great army for him to lead into this northern territory, later called Nuevo Mejico, in search of these seven cities of Cibola and their treasure.

After three days of Easter *fiesta* in Compostela, Mexico, Coronado set out with 700 horsemen, gaily plumed and caparisoned. Following these were many foot-soldiers, ox-carts, and two ships filled with provisions. These vessels were to sail up the Gulf of California and then up the rivers to keep in advance of the army; but this was not accomplished, for the rivers were not found navigable. Also there were droves of cattle and herds of sheep

Taos Pueblo Mission

to feed the army, and two priests to bless the expedition. One of these priests was Fray Juan de Padilla.

For over two years Coronado with his men made a fruitless search for gold and silver. They explored the whole country from the Grand Canyon on the west to what is now Rice County, Kansas, on the east and as far north as Colorado. At last he abandoned his search and returned to Mexico. All his followers who were still alive returned with him, except the two priests. They decided to remain to convert the Indians. Fray Luis de Escalona went to Pecos, now ruins near Santa Fe, where he was soon killed. Fray Juan de Padilla set out to return to the land of the Quivirans (now Kansas), where he had spent the former winter with Coronado; but on his way he was martyred.

About half a century later, in 1598, Nuevo Mejico, which vaguely included everything from the Pecos River to southern California, was colonized.

After this the Pueblo Indians endured the tyranny of Spanish rule for nearly a century. Then, in 1680, they rose in revolt, led by a half-Indian, half-Spaniard, named Popé, who lived in the Indian pueblo of San Juan de los Caballeros.

There had been many efforts, during those intervening years, to get the Indians to rebel in concerted action, but all had failed. These Indians were peace-loving, and the inhabitants of each village were suspicious of those of another pueblo. They lived in eighty villages, scattered over what is now New Mexico and Arizona, speaking five different dialects; each group not understanding the language of the others. There were no animals to furnish means of communication between the villages, since they possessed only dogs and turkeys, so that messages had to be carried by runners. When the inhabitants of a pueblo fared far from home, they encountered hostile Indians; especially if they ventured far enough to hunt buffaloes east of the Pecos, where usually they were attacked and partially or wholly annihilated by Commanches, Utes, Navajos, or Apaches. They feared outsiders and did not even trust other pueblos. Popé might have failed, too, but for his cleverness and an intense bitterness against the Spaniards, which had arisen among these Indians. Popé knew that the Indians' burden of oppression had received a last straw.

According to tradition, the "last straw," which lighted the final flame of rebellion, was the entombment of a group of Indian slaves. A shaft in a silver mine in the Ortiz mountains, near Santa Fe, caved in, entrapping alive these Pueblo Indians, who had been forced to work there. This so angered all the pueblos that they were willing to listen to Popé.

The "last straw" may have been another incident. Popé's efforts followed the historic killing
by the Spaniards of forty-seven prominent Indian
men, known as caciques, in 1675. These Indians,
important in their villages, were tried in Spanish
courts in Santa Fe for alleged witchcraft. They
were convicted of sorcery and were shot. This
slaughter may have been the "last straw," or perhaps both occurrences were more than the Indians
could bear.

Popé began at Taos. From pueblo to pueblo he
went, with two secret helpers.

The Pueblo Indians are always in need of rainfall. To them the clouds are sacred, as bringers of
rain. The Great Creative Force, or "Great Spirit,"
which, to the Indian, is both male and female and
works in rhythms, manifests itself in many forms.
These forms or spirits are called katcinas. There
are katcinas that pile the clouds; katcinas that make
seeds sprout; katcinas that cause growth; katcinas
that punish naughty children; katcinas that teach
little boys to hunt and little girls to grind corn;
katcinas who fashion the rainbow; katcinas that
bless homes; and many others. During the year, the
Indians have pageants to act out these things that
the katcinas do. For instance, at Christmas time
there are four days of Indian ceremony—we call
them "Indian dances"—to make the sun stop go-

ing southward as it sets along the horizon, to call
it back northward for another warm season. In
these pageants, Indian men put great masks made
of buckskin over their heads. The masks are decorated with symbols to show whether they represent
katcinas of growth, katcinas of cloud-making, or
some other katcinas representing other hidden
forces of nature. When a man puts on such a mask,
the Indians believe that, for the time he wears the
mask, the man really and truly becomes that sacred
being. They treat him with reverence and regard
him as a part of the Great Creative Force.

So Popé took with him two Indian men, with
rain-bringing katcina masks. These men he left
hidden outside each village as he went in to
call together the council in one of their kivas
—the underground chambers for special meetings
and for the performance of secret rites. Popé had
discovered a herb which, when thrown upon the
open fire, created a dense cloud of white smoke,
like piled cumulus clouds.

Blackness would wrap the pueblo in its star-
studded blanket. Deep listening quiet would settle
over it. Closely-shut mud houses would hug the
earth tighter in fear of things unseen, yet felt.
Their doors would open, then close quickly, to let
out men pulling blankets more protectingly about
them, hiding beneath these blankets from the

witches all about them, leering in the darkness.
With soft moccasins crunching the hard clay earth,
each hurried to the kiva and climbed down its
ladder, whose log poles pointed up toward the
Rain-bringers. At the foot of the ladder was the
fire pit, protected on three sides by upright stone
slabs. Some little sticks of piñon or juniper burned
there and sent up through the entrance hole a
smoke smelling of incense, to purify the men as
they climbed down through it. Beside the fire sat
the oldest men, rolling tobacco into strips of clean
husk for cigarettes, which only the older men, who
had reached the age of wisdom, could smoke. One
by one the others came to sit cross-legged upon the
clay floor, first round the wall where they could
lean back smudging their shoulder-blades with its
whitewash. Then they filled in the open space in
the center. In the leaping flames of the firelight,
their shadows danced ghoulishly upon the circular
wall. Faintness of light darkened their forms and
their intense bronze faces to the grayness of second
rows of shadows; still, sculptured shadows, not
dancing fantastically like those on the wall.

When all were at length assembled, Popé ad-
dressed them. Then he secretly threw his herb
upon the fire. White smoke poured out, filling the
chamber. Down the ladder, through this smoke,
appeared miraculously two sacred katcinas, more

holy than ever because they had come in a sacred
cloud. They would then speak to the Indians,
urging them to take up arms and drive away
the Spaniards if they wanted to retain their fields,
keep their streams of water, save their lives, and
their women and children from slavery and, finally,
if they desired the katcinas to send them rain.

Convinced by Popé's device that the Great Crea-
tors had commanded, the Indians promised to take
up arms against their conquerors. Once again Popé
would call the sacred cloud, which would come and
take away the katcinas. Then he would leave with
the villagers a rope of sinew tied into a given number of knots, with the instruction that each day a
knot should be untied. And upon the day of the
last knot, the Indians should slay or drive away all
Spaniards, beginning with the destruction of their
priest.

Popé enjoined the closest secrecy upon the Indians. He killed his own son-in-law, the Governor
of San Juan pueblo, believing him to be disloyal.
He allowed no women to know of the plans. Even
with all these precautions, several Indians, friendly
to the Spaniards, betrayed the plot. So Popé was
forced to call the uprising three days in advance
of the appointed time.

Many of the priests were martyred, missions were
partly burned, Spanish ranchers were slain, and the

Indians then attacked the remaining Spaniards in the old palace of the governors in Santa Fe, to which place the fleeing Spaniards had come for refuge. Entrenched behind its heavy walls, the Spaniards withstood the siege of the Indians for about seven days, but finally, when the Indians succeeded in cutting off their water supply, they were forced to retreat. The peace-loving Pueblos stood in the plaza and watched them go without harming them. The Indians followed the retreating Spanish for seventy miles to be sure that the intruders were really leaving; then the Indians took possession of Santa Fe. There they enjoyed an orgy of destruction of all things Spanish. They burned archives and bathed themselves thoroughly with suds made from the oily roots of yucca, or amole, to wash away the Christian baptism.

However, Indians of Isleta pueblo had been in most cordial and sympathetic relations with the Spaniards. They took in the refugees as these traveled southward. They housed them for a time and gave them fresh provisions. So when the white men continued their retreat, the Isleta Indians followed them. Because of their friendliness to the Spaniards, they were afraid to stay behind. Going southward, they established the village of Isleta del Sur near the Texas Indians. While there they learned from these Texans of the slaying of Fray

Padilla many years before, and of the burial of the priest in a cave, where his remains had become mummified in the dryness.

"We have seen the dried-up padre in the cave," claimed one of the Texas group. "Some day we will take you Isletans to see it," he promised.

But in 1692, before the promise had been fulfilled, Don Diego de Vargas Zapata Lujan Ponce de León led the Spaniards back north and retook the territory of Nuevo Mejico. Most of the Isleta Indians again followed the Spaniards; this time northward to re-establish their old village. At once they set to work to restore the partially destroyed mission. Then, it is said, the Indians held a council because the earth, where they used to plant, had become hard and white and their corn would not grow.

"The corn will not grow because we did not go to find the body of Fray Padilla," said one of the Indians. "If his body is still lying in that cave, his spirit is still walking on this earth. He is angry because we have left him among his enemies. So long as he is angry, our corn will not grow."

"That is true," said another. "We must send scouts to get the dried body of Fray Padilla and bring it here for proper burial."

"He must be buried in the church, the way the

white men bury their priests. That is what his spirit
will like," agreed a third.

And so, the village cacique sent men to find and
bring to Isleta the mummified body of Fray Padilla.
There with due ceremony he was laid to rest at the
altar in the mission, in a coffin made by hollowing
out a log of cottonwood and fitting it with a lid.

The corn began to grow; peace was made with
the Spaniards by the other Indian villagers, and a
live priest came to live at Isleta, and Fray Padilla
was forgotten.

Years later sickness came to the pueblo of Isleta.
Men, women, and children were dying. The Indians went into the church to pray to the God of
the white man, since their medicine men had failed
to drive away these witches of sickness from their
midst. Upon the ground floor of the mission they
knelt, chanting parts of the litany and telling their
Catholic beads.

Suddenly, in the midst of the chant, someone
gasped: "Look!" The nervous message was carried
on through the congregation, and all eyes became
centered upon the lid of Fray Padilla's coffin, slowly
appearing above the surface of the floor. The cacique with his counsellors went over and lifted the
lid. There lay the priest, just as he had been at the
time of burial. After crossing themselves, each rev-

erently tore off a small strip of his gray serge challis
as a keepsake. The members of the congregation
rushed forward to touch the padre in order to receive his blessing. Then reverently they redug his
grave to the depth of seven feet and buried him
again in the same spot. Immediately all of the sick
were cured.

Thereafter, whenever there was an excessive
drought, so that the corn would not grow, or sickness came again to the village, and the Indians went
into the church to pray, Fray Padilla's coffin would
rise above ground to bless the Indians and to
remedy their troubles. Each time he would be
deeply reburied.

At length, in 1889, the Indians had a dance in
the church, where a wooden floor had been laid.
They danced at night, without the consent of the
parish priest. Several Indian friends of the priest
stood at the altar rail to see that the sanctuary
should not be entered or profaned. When these
men had taken their position, from outside came
the sound of drum beats. Looking through the
open doorway, they saw the waning moon peeping
big and lopsided above the horizon. In a moment
the dancers came into the moonlit churchyard,
some silhouetted against the moon. There were per-
sonified deer, antelopes, mountain sheep, and buffaloes. With sticks for forelegs and appropriate

horns or antlers upon their heads, these actors came
with prancing steps into the center of the nave,
followed by a chorus of men, swathed in many-
hued Indian blankets and carrying four big drums,
hewn from logs and decorated with V-shaped strips
of turquoise, black, white, and red. The dim
candle-light softened and harmonized the colors
and lent its feeling of mystery, as if one were about
to hear voices and see scenes from a sphere beyond
one's own. The deep voices, rumbling with stac-
cato accent rather than singing, and the deep-
toned drum beats echoed and re-echoed among
the age-stained carved beams and corbels above.

The animals danced back and forth, as the so-
norous din increased in volume. Then there was
a knocking on the church floor, louder than the
singing and the prancing of feet and sharper than
the drum-beats. The altar moved up and down to
its rhythm. The guardians of the altar, who had
been standing like a row of blanketed statues, each
tightly swathed except for slits through which
shone their black eyes, went to see who was playing
this sacrilegious trick. They could find no one
there. But in a moment the knocking and the rock-
ing of the altar occurred again. The men ripped
up a board from the floor and discovered that it
was Fray Padilla's coffin knocking there.

One of them called out: "Fray Padilla is knocking. He does not like this dancing in the church."

Panic at once spread among all those present, and, with pushing and shoving, the excited audience left the church, each rushing to the safety of his own home, afraid of the displeasure of so magical a priest.

At this time New Mexico was becoming more thickly settled by immigrants from the eastern states, and there was so much discussion throughout the state about these claims of the Isleta Indians, that in 1895 Archbishop Chapelle, then of the Archdiocese of Santa Fe, ordered an investigation. With the permission of the Indians, a group of priests, a doctor, and four Indians exhumed the body of the buried priest for examination. Although the corpse had been so recently reburied, "deep enough to cover a man standing upright," according to the Indians, the coffin was found flush with the floor of the Church, and the body was just as the Indians had said it would be. The corpse was mummified, with a long black beard and long hair. It wore a stole of color once purple, and there were rents in the serge challis into which fitted the pieces in the possession of several old Indians.

After examination the body was re-entombed in the sanctuary near the altar, one foot deep.

An old Indian, then ninety years of age, testified before this committee, that the body had appeared above ground when he was a young man, about the year 1830. Although he did not see it at the time of this investigation, he described it from memory, just as the committee had found it. At that time (1830) Fray Padilla had "cured a sickness."

Three other Indians testified that the coffin appeared the next time about 1845, when the Indians again needed a blessing.

Pablo Abeyta, an outstanding figure in Isleta today, testified that he was one of the guardians of the altar in 1889, at the time of the dance in the church.

Fray Padilla's last appearance was on the night of December 24, 1914. The Indians, having forgotten their former reprimand, danced again in the church. This ceremony followed the celebration of midnight Mass on Christmas Eve, after the parish priest had retired. It was bitterly cold. Against the whitewashed walls were row on row of eyes set in slits of bronze flesh, the rest of the faces and bodies being encased in wrapped blankets of candle-softened colors. The rows of eyes were broken occasionally by the appearance of two uncovered heads: the front one heavily fringed with black bangs and side-locks, and the small one behind, black-crowned, lolling in sleep. Back of these, black shadows danced in fitful candlelight, since each of the few flames also danced in the breeze from the open doors.

In the center was the row of men dancers. Their long, flowing black hair was dotted with wisps of cotton and crowned with a tuft of parrot feathers. Their bodies glistened with colored grease paint, and they shook gourd rattles, emphasizing the strokes with stamping of fur-tipped moccasins. As they twirled at intervals, short kilts and long-tasseled sashes rippled in arcs. Suddenly, above the syncopated stamping and the rattling, there was a knocking upon the floor beside the altar. Someone whispered, "Fray Padilla!" Immediately in panic, all of the Indians rushed out, pushing one another and pressing against the babies on the mothers' backs; these little forms, spraddle-legged, were clearly outlined under the tight blankets that held them. The Indians knew that the spirit of the priest was reproaching them for defiling his sanctuary. Sure enough, when they ripped up the floor boards, the coffin was there flush with the floor. Fray Padilla was again re-buried. Many of the Indians believe that he will come again. So say the bells at Isleta, when they call the Indians to Mass.

One of the priests to investigate the rising of Fray Padilla was Father Antonio Docher, who

died in Albuquerque about 1928. For many years
he was stationed at Isleta, where he coaxed a lovely
garden to blossom in the arid sands of his patio.
He also had charge of three little missions nearby:
Los Lunas, Los Lentes, and Los Pajaritos. Father
Docher had great abiding faith in the scapular. He
not only wore one around his neck, but he always
carried another about with him in a small case.
More than once these scapulars performed miracles for him. At one time the miracle occurred at
Los Lentes.

The Staying of the Flood Waters

FATHER DOCHER was spending the night in his room adjoining the mission of Los Lentes. The mission was built between a large irrigation ditch and the Rio Grande. The land was low and flat. Along the ditch, willows grew like a long barometric snake changing color with the seasons, from gray green to deep green and finally from russet to rich wine color. Along the river giant cottonwoods towered. Their great trunks stood knotted and twisted as if wrung dry by some giant hand and then allowed to partly unwrap, while their wide branching limbs rose in supplication to that mighty wringing hand above.

Clouds had been piling all about the landscape. Father Docher asked one of the natives: "Will it rain tonight?"

The man answered: "One cannot tell."

It did rain. A terrific storm blew up. A storm that at first raged farther up the river. The wind had been howling and the rain had been clattering for some time when men of the village came running to pound upon the door of the padre.

"Come quickly, Father," called the men; "there

24

is a flood. The church will soon be swept away. You will drown. The river has broken its banks, and is flowing down the ditch and all across the land between. It will be here in a moment. Come quickly, Father."

Father Docher ran out. The men were soaked and muddy. Each carried a spade or hoe, with which he had been trying to mend the breaks along the river and stem the tide of water. The father could hear the cruel hissing and foaming of unruly waters. By the light of the men's lanterns he could see it rushing across the land. Hastily he stepped forward and threw his scapular into the raging stream. The scapular floated upon the current, which promptly rushed back into the river bed and flowed away in its regular course. The mission was saved. To the old-timers of Los Lentes, the bell rings out this story when it summons them to Mass.

Another time the mission at Los Pajaritos caught fire, when there was no one present to help put out the flames. Father Docher drew off his scapular and threw it into the fire, extinguishing the flames at once.

During a storm one night at Los Lunas, the bells of the church began ringing violently. Men of the village jumped from their beds, snatched up clothing, and ran out.

"What is it?" asked one. "What is wrong?" "What is the matter?" All spoke at the same time.

In excited confusion, half-dressed and half-drenched, men ran toward the clanging bells. They found a torrent of water sweeping through the church. The flood had already carried away the priest's vestments and, by swishing in strong current against the walls, it was beginning to inundate them. The church would soon collapse.

Seizing the image of their patron saint (St. Anthony) from his niche, the men carried it out into the storm. At once the elements quieted. The waters subsided. This incident was often told by Father Docher. When the church bells toll, they also tell this same tale; but never again have the bells rung as they rang out that night.

The Isleta mission is not as old as the mission at Zia pueblo, which was built about 1600. At that time the village of Zia had around 2,500 inhabitants. Today the number of Indians has dwindled to scarcely more than a hundred, yet the old church still stands with its massive mud walls, as a memorial to those days of advanced Pueblo Indian culture. It is dedicated to Our Lady of the Assumption.

Recently mysterious little people at Zia have, among other performances, played the organ in the mission on certain days at noon.

The Jinxes of Zia

THESE little people might be called the jinxes of Zia. They are real, like "little dolls" or pixies, although they are never seen or heard by anyone except the Indian children. These youngsters rush, with eyes stretched wide in excitement, to bring tales of the "little witches" to their parents.

One little Indian boy was left for a short time to watch the irrigation water running in his father's corn patch, while the father went home on an errand. When the parent returned, he found the little fellow sprawling in the shallow ditch of running water, nearly drowned because he could not keep his face out of the water, unable to get up and weeping with fright.

"A *choogy-ay*," he screamed, "pushed me down into the ditch."

"Perhaps you stubbed your toe," said the father.

"No," insisted the child; "it was a little man like a doll. I saw him. He is a little witch, a *choogy-ay*."

Several little girls had been hearing the playing

of the melodeon in the mission at noon. One day they slipped over just before noon to peep through the church windows to see the musician. Soon little people came from behind the altar. They climbed up on the organ keys and began running along them, making the keys play as they ran.

The youngest child in the group made a dash toward the church door. Thinking she had been charmed in some way by the strange little people, the other little girls in panic caught her.

"Why were you going into the church?" asked one child.

"I want to get one of those little dolls to play with," replied the other, now in tears of disappointment.

When the children slipped back to the window, the music had ceased and the dolls were gone.

Though none of the grown-up Indians has seen or heard the "little dolls," they believe implicitly in their existence and in the tales the children tell about them.

The collector of these legends, with her Zia artist friend, is accused of being directly responsible for all these pranks of the little witches.

Eighteen years ago, the collector first heard hints of little creatures with long red tongues, about whom there were many tales. Time and time again, she tried to persuade Indian friends to tell

her about these little people. Some of these Indians would only giggle and shake their heads;
others would shake their heads and set their
mouths into a thin, tight line; while still others
would look frightened, with eyes stretched wide
and breath shortened. At last, weary of persistent
requests, several friends told about the *choogy-ays,*
or "little witches." They told the tales with the
warning that, since the *choogy-ays* were being
talked about, they would surely begin playing
their impish pranks. Elizabeth laughed at this.
She was amused.

She persuaded a young Indian artist of Zia
pueblo to come and draw pictures of *choogy-ays,*
while she wrote down the stories. He came. Then
the troubles commenced. Daily, as she wrote part
time and he drew, the mishaps began: wrong groc-
eries were delivered; new shoe strings broke, sew-
ing threads insisted upon snarling and breaking;
punctures came in new tires; the carburetor sprung
a mysterious leak at midnight, far from home; the
telephone would not ring, would not work; elec-
tric bulbs blinked out; potted plants dropped from
holders and crashed; and so on and so on. One mishap seemed to follow another. Each time the artist
almost fell from his chair with laughter. He would
say, "It's the *choogy-ays.*" And at his pueblo of
Zia, the pranks began to be played upon the chil-

dren. The artist was called home to the village by the old men. They held a junta, a meeting, and decided that the pictures of the little witches must be destroyed and that the artist must be banished from the village for an indefinite time. He had to move to the white man's city, where he is still living.

Near Zia pueblo and also near the town of Bernalillo are several Indian and other missions. It is about one of these churches that the legend of the burned Missal is told. The scorched Mass book is said to have been preserved. Although the legend is almost identical with an old Irish tradition, it is told in all seriousness as having happened in "one of the churches near Bernalillo, perhaps the Indian church at Santa Ana." The tale is known in New Mexico as *La Mano Negra*. All the church bells near Bernalillo ring out this story.

La Mano Negra

THE elderly priest, who had for years been in charge of the missions near Bernalillo, having them as out-missions, was not well for some years before his death. During those years he received many stipends for celebrating Mass for the souls in purgatory. Feeling ill and tired, he had failed to celebrate many of these Masses, although he had kept the offerings for so doing. When he died, these omissions lay heavily upon his conscience, so that his soul could not rest in peace.

After his death, on several different nights at midnight, some of the Indians of the village heard a bell ringing inside the church, the little bell that always had called them to Communion. Each was afraid to mention it, for fear the other Indians would think he had been bewitched.

But José, a friend of the sacristan, could stand the suspense no longer. He went to find him.

"Have you been ringing the little bell in the church that calls us to Communion?" he asked.

"No," replied the sacristan. "Have you heard the bell, too?"

José nodded.

"Then I have not been mistaken," said the sacristan. "After I had heard it three times, I slipped on my moccasins and went into the church to see what was happening there; but the church was dark and empty. I could find no one, and the bell was in its place when I felt for it."

"When I heard it again the next night, I thought I was bewitched," added the sacristan after a pause, adjusting the gay blanket that was over his shoulders. "But if you also have heard it, José, then there is something going on in the church every night, or both of us have been bewitched."

"We must go and see," said José. "As soon as it is dark, I will meet you at the church door and we will wait inside until the bell rings to find out who is ringing it." He walked away with his moccasins making soft, precise thuds and straight-pointed tracks on the dust-coated clay.

The two men met as agreed and sat in the dark church waiting. With striped blankets drawn tightly around them, outlining shoulders and buttocks, they crouched against the cold church wall, like two pygmies in its vastness, making themselves as nearly as possible into balls to conserve the heat of their bodies. As their eyesight grew accustomed to the pitch darkness, the window high in the wall of the transept took on a shaded outline. Every so often one of them would softly grunt to receive an acknowledged grunt in return, for assurance that the eerieness was not witchery. Once the sacristan, who was growing old, nodded, but the tickle of his hooped earrings against his cheek awakened him with a start. Muscles cramped, but the watchers shifted them as seldom and as little as possible so as not to break the stillness, not to interfere with their quest. At last, when each felt he could bear the ache of squatting no longer, an apparition appeared at the altar. There was a luminosity surrounding the appearance, that allowed the Indians to see clearly their former priest, looking as he had appeared in life. Opening the Missal, he went through the celebration of the Mass. Then he looked about for his acolyte to ring the bell for Communion. There was no acolyte, so he rang the bell himself. Then, finding no one at the altar rail, the priest went away again into the darkness.

Awed by what they had seen, José and the sacristan shuffled themselves up, shook the stiffness from their legs, and went out of the church in silence. Outside they stopped.

"Did you see the padre celebrate the Mass?" asked José.

"Yes," replied the sacristan. "And the padre did not believe in witches, so we are not bewitched.

But I cannot understand how he can be here, since I buried him myself. We must speak to the cacique and the councilmen."

And so at a meeting in the house of the cacique, José and the sacristan told what they had seen. "What does it mean?" they asked. But the old men shook their heads.

"We must go see," said one.

"Yes," said others.

"We might tell it to some of our Mexican friends. It is their religion. They might know what it means," suggested another.

But the Mexicans were also baffled and unbelieving. So it was arranged that a group of both Indians and their Mexican neighbors should watch again in the church that next night. As they crouched or sat on the cold church floor in the darkness, the Indians were perturbed by the restlessness and frequent movements of the Mexicans. They were afraid the priest would not come if there were noise, but although the Indians sat like silent statues, this was not impressed upon their neighbors, who startled the stillness with the clearing of throats and several times there was even whispering among the few Mexican women present.

But the priest came, and the sight stilled the audience. He celebrated the Mass and picked up

the bell to ring it. But at the first tinkle an over-
wrought woman screamed at the sound.

Turning in surprise, the padre placed his hand
upon the open Missal to steady himself, and seeing the living people present, his apparition faded
from sight. And he has never been seen from that
day to this. Nor has anyone heard the bell ring.

Next day, when the sacristan went into the
church, he discovered that the priest's hand had
scorched its shape through several pages of the
Missal, making *la mano negra,* the black hand,
upon the Mass book.

Another of these early missions, one westward
from Bernalillo, is the remarkable mission at
Acoma pueblo. This village has been called The
City of the Sky because it is perched on top of a
great, bare, wind-swept rock over 350 feet above
the surrounding plain.

This mission was built about 1629 by Fray Ramirez and the Indians. According to some authori-
ties, the present building is not the original
church, which they think was destroyed during
the Pueblo Rebellion, but is one built after the
retaking of New Mexico in 1692. At any rate, the
mission is a remarkable edifice, when one appreci-
ates the fact that all the lumber for its construc-
tion was brought on the backs of Indian men from
San Mateo mountain (Mt. Taylor) twenty miles

away, and that the church was forty-five years in the building, even the clay for making the adobe bricks having been hauled up from the plain below.

There are three extraordinary tales connected with this mission at Acoma. One is associated with the coming of Fray Juan Ramirez; a second concerns a portrait of San José, which was given to Acoma by the friar; and a third is about strange noises heard in the *convento* adjoining the church. So to each listener, the Acoma chimes tell a different tale.

The Reception of Fray Ramirez
at Acoma

IN THE early days Acoma was not friendly toward the Spaniards. Because of its strategic position, it was a difficult stronghold for the Spaniards to take in conquering the country. Oñate left a number of soldiers encamped at the foot of its mesa to stay and take possession of the village. These were under the command of Don Juan Saldivar, a favorite nephew of Oñate.

One night, under cover of darkness, Saldivar and five other officers succeeded in scaling the cliff and reaching the village by cleverly throwing a short log across a deep fissure in the mesa. At daybreak they were discovered by the Acomans. The Indians killed Saldivar and forced the others to leap over the edge of the precipice. Miraculously these escaped death.

Captain Saldivar's brother was so incensed over the captain's death that he gained permission from Oñate to mobilize every available soldier among the colonists at San Gabriel, Oñate's first capital, to attack Acoma. This was done on January 21, 1599, in one of the bloodiest battles in New Mexico history. The houses of the pueblo were burned and nearly all the Indians were killed. Then, it is said, Oñate or Saldivar ordered the amputation of the right foot of every Indian man left alive, with the exception of one visiting Indian from Hopiland. He was ordered home and, since he needed both feet for the journey, his right hand was cut off instead of his foot.

This battle so embittered the Acoma Indians that every priest coming to them for some years afterward was martyred. One priest, it is said, was carrying an umbrella because of the glare and heat of the sunshine. As he was forced to step off the edge of the cliff, he opened his umbrella and jumped. The umbrella proved a successful parachute. The priest made a safe landing below and got away alive.

Finally, in 1629, a young priest, Fray Juan Ramirez, felt himself especially called to minister to these Indians. Believing that by going to Acoma, the new priest was simply committing suicide, his colleagues tried to dissuade him, but Fray Ramirez was determined and set out alone upon his journey, accompanied by a burro loaded with his few belongings, his books, and the rolled canvas of an oil painting.

When he neared the foot of the mesa, a volley of arrows whizzed about him. The wind was blowing with such force that, although several arrows pierced his billowing brown robe, none entered his body. A row of angry brown faces appeared along the cliff far above him. But, driving his burro before him, the friar kept on his way. At that moment a small girl in the village above became overcurious. She went too near the edge and fell over, landing on a sandstone ledge near the friar. There she lay limp, and all supposed she had been killed.

Fray Ramirez ran to her. Finding that she was merely unconscious, he lifted her in his arms and began to ascend the difficult sandy trail, greatly impeded by his burden. It took a long time. The Indians, from above, saw the child stir in the priest's arms. They laid aside their bows and arrows, thinking that a miracle had been performed. When the priest reached the top, they received him. Later the friar had the Indians build a trail for burros, where he had climbed. The Indians still call it *El Camino del Padre* ("The Road of the Father"), but, because of the depth of sand lying upon it, the trail has been of little use except for a few animals.

Fray Ramirez must have been a most able and astute man. He not only accomplished the almost impossible feat of building a great adobe mission on top of a windswept mesa of solid rock, where all material had to be brought up from the plain below on the backs of Indians and a few burros, but he taught the Indians improved methods of farming. He was useful in many ways. He also gave to them for the church the canvas he had brought with him, a fine painting of San José (St. Joseph), which had come from Spain and which many people believe was painted by one of the great masters who went to Spain to help decorate the Escorial for Philip II, perhaps El Greco.

When Fray Ramirez died as an old man, the Indians believed that his spirit entered this portrait of San José, which he had loved and before which he had knelt for so many hours each day, telling his beads. It became very sacred.

This painting, over two centuries later, won fame in the courts of New Mexico in a case entitled Pueblo of Laguna v. Pueblo of Acoma.

Zia Mission

Pueblo of Laguna versus Pueblo
of Acoma

SHORTLY before 1699 some of the Indians of Acoma, which had become over-populated because of the good agricultural teachings of Fray Ramirez, extended their lands beyond the fields then cultivated by other Acomans. In order to have water for irrigating these new corn patches, they dammed up the little San José river to form a lake. Then, to be nearer their fields, these Indians moved to a rock bluff above the lake, where they were joined by Indians from Zia, Zuni, and other nearby pueblos, forming the pueblo of Laguna (Lake).

It is said that, although these cultivated fields of Laguna adjoined the fields of Acoma, the crops never flourished as they did for Acoma. Finally, almost as late as 1800, the Laguna Indians decided that their lack of success was because they did not have the blessings of Fray Ramirez, whose spirit was in the painting of San José. They determined to borrow the painting or to steal it. Which one they did, no one knows. At any rate, they came into possession of the painting. When Acoma came to take it back again, the Lagunas met them with guns and drove them away. Then was displayed an interesting bit of Indian psychology. Acoma's crops failed, and Laguna's flourished. Knowing that the spirit, that they thought had blessed their fields—the spirit of Fray Ramirez embodied in the painting of San José—was not present to consecrate the fields, the Acomans did not work, and consequently their harvest failed. But at Laguna, the Indians worked diligently, feeling that their crops had received that blessing.

For over half a century Laguna kept the painting in its mission with an armed guard always on watch over it. Laguna flourished in every way during those years, while Acoma became more and more impoverished.

At length, the Acomans became desperate. There was no need for the women to make big pots, for there were too few seeds to save. But to forget their hunger, women spent long hours over their pottery, covering them with fine, decorative designs of cloud symbols, sacred parrots that might talk to the katcinas, fancy seed pods and flourishing leaves. The men spent far too much time squatting in the sunshine, making their long-fringed, tight buckskin leggings bag at knees and dry out to stiffness. They knew that Laguna had a much stronger armed force than they could muster, but they determined in any event to fight rather than starve to death.

The same priest was at that time in charge of both villages. He learned of Acoma's intention to fight and knew the folly of it. Going to Laguna, he induced the Indians there to send a delegation with him to Acoma, taking with them the painting of San José. There they would celebrate Mass in the mission in the presence of the saint. Afterward the priest would place a number of slips of paper in a basket, with one slip bearing the likeness of St. Joseph. These would be drawn by a representative from each pueblo. To the side drawing this picture would belong the painting of San José.

"Since this basket," concluded the priest, "will be blessed by the celebration of Mass and will lie at the feet of the saint, in the presence of the spirit of Fray Ramirez and of God, the drawing by lot will show the divine will in settling this dispute."

It was done as the priest said. The Indians, dressed as for *fiesta,* the men in woven cotton jackets and fringed buckskin leggings, the women in black woolen *mantas,* contrasting with the whiteness of freshly cleaned buckskin leggings. The long black hair of all hung with glossy sheen

from recent shampoo with yucca suds. Upon the
clay floor of the great bare nave of the mission,
they knelt. Above them extended the high mud
walls. High up the walls reached the tremendous
carved beams. In a shaft of sunlight, piercing the
dimness, from one of the small, high windows,
stood the priest in coarse brown cassock and rope
cincture, and a young Indian girl dressed like the
women. The young girl, Margarita, drew for Laguna, and the priest, Father Lopez, represented
Acoma.

The fifth slip bore the likeness of the saint and
was drawn by the priest.

The delegation from Laguna refused to accept
this decision. Their long black bangs and the
wrapped coils of hair at the nape of their necks
shook with indignation, swinging the big silver
loops or turquoise drops hanging from flabby
bronze lobes of their ears. Seizing their guns, they
let their gaily colored blankets drop from their
shoulders about their waists. With quick, short
steps, the toe of each moccasin pointing precisely
ahead, as if they walked upon an invisible rope,
they rushed to the altar to carry away their painting.

The Acomans, with faces more shriveled and
parched, like dried peppers, because of their short-

age of food, wished to resist, but the priest persuaded them of the uselessness of such a move. Laguna once more took away the painting.

Dispute and trouble continued between the two villages. At last Father Lopez encouraged the Indians to take their case to the courts of the new Government, that of the United States, which had been set up over the territory of New Mexico. It is said that the Indians spent all their hard-earned communal savings to pay lawyers' fees. The case was first tried in the district court and then appealed to the supreme court of the territory in January, 1857, where it is recorded as the twenty-sixth case.

The supreme court of New Mexico decided that the painting belonged to Acoma and should be returned to that pueblo. In the judge's opinion as handed down, he states that the testimony of the first witness, Quanico, proved that the painting belonged to Acoma. He gives as one of the reasons for his decision that it had been shown that "unless San José is in Acoma the people thereof cannot prevail with God."

When the Acomans went home with the good news, a group of them set out for Laguna to get the painting. They found it leaning against a juniper tree halfway between the two villages.

They will tell you today that San José was so happy over going home again that he had come of his own accord and met them halfway.

Now the third story of this mission at Acoma relates to a curious phenomenon, strange noises in the *convento*.

The Voices in the Convent at Acoma

SOME years ago a young architect had an appointment with the priest who was then in charge of the mission at Acoma. They were to meet at Acoma to discuss the much needed restoration of parts of the old mission.

Delays upon the road prevented the young man and his companions from reaching Acoma until sundown of the appointed day. Since the priest was expecting him, he left his companions to camp at the foot of the mesa and set out to climb to the village. In the semi-darkness the natural stairway, in a crevice of the cliff wall leading up, was particularly difficult of ascent. The young man felt chagrined that a belated Indian woman, in front of him, climbed with ease in her skimp skirt, though she carried a burden upon her head, while he mounted with great effort, slipping, grabbing, and panting as he went.

It was the eve of the celebration of their patron saint's day, the feast of St. Stephen. When he reached the top, fires were burning in outdoor ovens here and there, getting ready for the morrow's early baking. They sent weird reflections against dusk-covered mud walls, lit here and there by splashes of square lights from tiny windows, like massive jack-o'-lanterns close to the sky holding revelry and jeering at the black expanse of all the earth far below.

From one of these houses an Indian man came out, demanding curtly: "What do you want? What are you doing here?" But when told that the father was expecting him, the Indian immediately changed his mien and offered to conduct the young man to the *convento,* where he would find the padre.

In the strange quiet of an Indian village at dusk, broken only by the uncanny rumble of muffled drum beats, sounding now and again to emphasize the hush, the two circled round the irregular piles of houses, across a stretch of wind-swept rock, toward the massive mission, silhouetted, with its soft-lined belfries, against a darkening sky, like a great owl with its two listening ears.

In the doorway of the long *convento,* adjoining the church, a rectangle of candlelight haloed the shadowlike form of the priest, standing in greeting in his Franciscan robes.

"It is too late," he said, "for you to see the mission tonight, but you may get a glimpse of the condition of the walls with my flashlight."

Whereupon the priest threw the rays of his light along the façade of the church and on along the wall of the cemetery. Every ten feet along this wall a sculptured face grinned grotesquely, like old Mayan carvings. It is a custom of Acoma to model these faces in preparation for their saint's day dance. Being of adobe, they soon weather away. That night the faces were fresh and gruesome. The eeriness of the whole experience, since his climb to the mesa, was a fit setting for the next remark of the priest, as they went into the house.

"You don't mind sleeping in a haunted room, do you?" he asked. The long, moving shadows in the candle-lit room, danced to emphasize his words.

"Not if you sleep there with me," replied the guest.

Then, as they had supper in the middle of the three rooms, all in a row, comprising the *convento,* the priest told this story.

Before his time, there had been a Jesuit priest in charge of the mission at Acoma. In the middle of the night, when he was asleep in the bedroom of the *convento,* he heard the murmur of excited voices in the distance. When he listened closely he found that they seemed to come from the cloister. Then the sound drew nearer. It was like a babel of voices, sighing, moaning, and chattering in un-

usual excitement. Suddenly the noise grew thunderous, and the priest was snatched from his bed by an unseen force and hurled out through the door to the terrace. Picking himself up, the priest decided that he must have had some strange and terrible nightmare, but he still could not understand why he had found himself lying on the terrace.

Some time later the same experience was repeated. This time the priest knew that it could not be a dream. He felt assured that it was the work of the devil and concluded that he was not wanted any longer at Acoma. Therefore he asked for a transfer to a new field of labor. This was granted.

"Since then," concluded the father, "nothing more has been heard of the voices. I have slept in the same room, where we shall sleep tonight, many times, but I have never been haunted."

Late that night the two went to bed. The priest had a small bedstead suspended from the rafters by ropes, "because of the rats," he explained. Beside this was a cot upon which the young man was to sleep. But sleep he could not. The day had been too long, too full of adventure, with digging his car wheels out of deep sand and off high centers, viewing the majesty of Acoma mesa towering rugged and high above the deep-rutted country below, with its sister mesa, "Enchanted Mesa," nearby, narrower and taller, more austere than itself. He recalled the story of this enchanted mesa.

Long ago the ancestors of these Acoma Indians had lived there. It was more protected from enemies, for there was only one way of ascent and descent from its lofty top. The Indians went up and down this perilous pathway to grow their food (corn, squash, and beans) and their cotton. It was harvest time. All the people, young and old, were needed to gather the fruits, for it had been a good, rainy year. One morning at dawn all went gaily forth to garner. Mothers carried wee babies tightly held in cotton blankets upon their backs. Fathers helped toddling ones. Men, women, and children climbed down singing in unison as they went, the women in treble, one octave higher than the rumbling bass. All set forth except a few very old men and women, who could no longer make the journey down the steep and perilous path.

In the early afternoon, clouds began piling along the horizon. Black and ominous, they rose and joined together in the zenith. From the sky, cut by vivid streaks of lightning, deep thunder rolled and a deluge of raindrops fell. The whole earth was soaked. A great avalanche of rock broke loose from Enchanted Mesa and fell with a crash below. It was the pathway that came tumbling. The Indians below stood aghast. Far above on the

rim of the cliff they saw the old people making
frantic gestures with their arms like tiny shriveled
gnomes. For days men tried in every way to reach
them. They could not scale the cliffs. They could
not get back to their homes. Finally, they were
forced to give up, to build new homes and to leave
the old people to perish. Then they built the present Acoma.

The young man thought of this as the unac-
customed silence of the Indian village kept him
awake. The stillness was heavy, broken only by
the gentle snoring of the sleeping priest. Some
time after midnight this silence was disturbed by
a rustling sound, like excited whispering coming
from the direction of the church. Soon the volume
of sound increased as if it were the agitated voices
of many people approaching nearer the room.
Then suddenly there was a breathless, oppressive
feeling in the room, followed immediately by the
explosive sound of the door slamming with terrific force. It had been left open. The awakened
priest sprang from his bed. The young man
jumped up. But only silence reigned again.

The two ran to the door, but it had been wedged
with such force into its casing that they could not
budge it, pulling with all their might. Even the
hinges were bent, it had been slammed with such
supernatural strength. For half an hour they

worked with tools to pry the door open. Finally, by removing the hinges and working more, they succeeded in disembedding it and thus they got outside.

There was nothing to be seen. The stillness of the dark village lay undisturbed. The Indians slept.

"Well, I guess we have experienced it," said the priest. "You have heard the voices that were heard by the Jesuit priest. Perhaps the closed door saved us from being thrown out of the room."

There was now no chance for sleep. The two men spent the rest of the night discussing the strange phenomenon.

Not only the bells of the Indian missions in the pueblos ring out their weird tales, but there are stories chimed by the bells in the churches built for the Spanish settlers themselves, or for the Mexican Indians who came with them.

The Bell of San Miguel Chapel

AN OLD bell stands mounted today within the chapel of San Miguel in Santa Fe. Once it hung in the belfry to summon to worship the Tlascalan Indians. These Indians had followed Oñate up from Old Mexico. The mission of San Miguel was built in their *barrio de Analco,* immediately across the small *rio de Santa Fe* from the Royal Village of the Holy Faith of St. Francis of Assisi, now called only Santa Fe ("Holy Faith"), which was occupied by the Spanish conquistadors themselves.

During a violent storm in 1872, the three towers of San Miguel fell with a crash, bringing down the bell with them. Only one of the towers was restored. Although buttresses were then built to support the weakened church walls, they were not considered strong enough to support the added 780-pounds weight of the bell. So it is now kept inside the nave of the church. The bell is four inches thick. It has a beautiful tone and bears upon it the inscription *San José ruega por nosotros* ("St. Joseph, pray for us"). It was a gift to the chapel by the Ortiz family.

The story is that the bell was cast in Spain in

1356. At that time the Moors had been in possession of almost the whole Spanish peninsula for over seven centuries, having gradually extended their dominion during all that time.

The inhabitants in a little Spanish village heard that the Moors were coming to take their village also. As was always the case in those days, when the people were in trouble they turned for counsel to the parish priest.

"If the Moors come to take away your homes, my children," said the priest, "it is because you have not attended Mass as you should. Make a bell in honor of St. Joseph, the patron of the home. Then we shall celebrate the Mass, asking St. Joseph to pray for us and we shall promise that every time his bell rings we will all obey its summons."

The villagers at once sent for a coppersmith to make the bell. When he arrived they held *fiesta*, dancing in the streets, dancing in the church, tossing flowers everywhere, serenading and feasting. Wine flowed freely. Women put on their finest silk dresses with flowing skirts and bedecked themselves in all their heavy gold jewelry. Men, with silver buckles and silver buttons, appeared in all their finery of satins and laces. *Fiesta* grew more and more hilarious in spirit, until one young woman ran to the molten metal forming the bell. Snatching off her golden jewelry, she called: "We shall make the bell *muy rico para San José.* The Moors cannot come." With that, she threw her jewels into the hot copper and iron. It was a dare to all the others. Men and women rushed to throw in their jewels, their buttons, the silver studdings from bridles and saddles. Older women came with silver plate from their houses. They sang and danced round the bell as it was being cast. This addition of precious metal caused the thickness of the bell and gave it its beautiful tone, so beautiful that it frightened away the approaching Moors.

Years later the bell was brought to Mexico and afterward came to New Mexico with the founder of the Ortiz family.

Another story rings out the bell of San Miguel chapel.

Making the Blind Man See

WHEN the Ortiz bell hung in the belfry at the San Miguel chapel, no one rang it at midday. The bells of the big church on the Santa Fe plaza would be rung at that time. Every day for a long time there came into the chapel at noon an old blind man.

He would come tap-tapping with his cane and kneel at the altar to pray to St. Cecilia, the patron of music, because he loved so to hear the chiming of the chapel bell. As he prayed, the bell would begin to ring of its own accord, with no one touching the bell rope. As it rang the old man would suddenly call out: "I can see! I can see!"

People began to follow him into church to witness the strange miracle. When they did so, the old man would describe to them everything in the church: "There is the painting of the saint showing only his head and breast—the one which the padre says has the name of Velasquez on the other side. There are holes in the canvas, where Indian arrows pierced it when our fathers carried the saint in procession. There on the side walls are the tin

57

sconces to hold the candles. There are the pictures of the stations of the cross, the prints that came from France. There is the great carved rafter supporting the choir loft and there beside the altar is the spot where they say De Vargas is buried." And so he would point out one thing and another, which he could see.

But as soon as the bell stopped ringing, blindness came upon him again. With his stick, the old man would shuffle away until the next noon hour. This practice he kept up until death finally released him from his blindness.

Since 1859 this chapel has been used as a college chapel in connection with St. Michael's College conducted by the Christian Brothers.

There is also in Santa Fe a school for young women founded, at the same time as St. Michael's, by the Sisters of Loretto. Upon their grounds is an interesting little Gothic chapel built of native red stone. A delightful belief persists in connection with the stairway leading to the choir loft in this little sanctuary. The following is the story tolled by its bells.

The Staircase of Loretto Chapel

ARCHBISHOP LAMY, a French priest who became the first archbishop of Santa Fe, made it one of his chief duties to establish schools in Santa Fe for the young Spanish boys and girls belonging to the distinguished old families, who previously had been obliged to send their children east, to Mexico or to Spain, for proper training in letters and in gentility. He wished to keep these young people at home. Therefore he sent for a group of Sisters of Loretto to join a caravan over the old Santa Fe trail. These frightened but dauntless sisters had many experiences while crossing the great stretches of prairie. Their caravan was attacked by Indians, was joined by bandits, and experienced all the other hardships of traveling in those early days. At length they reached Santa Fe and founded the academy of the Loretto Convent.

Next the Archbishop longed to build in his episcopal city a French church like the one he had attended as a boy in France. A chapel was also needed for the young ladies of the Loretto Academy. At last his dream was to be realized. He sent to Italy for stonecutters, since the natives of New Mexico could make only mud bricks, adobes. He sent east for a notable young architect to draw plans and to see that they were carried out.

The young man proved too charming. When the cathedral, except the belfries, was finished, but the little Loretto chapel was only just begun, he became involved in a triangular love affair and was shot and killed. There was no one to take his place, so the Archbishop had to turn over the completion of the little chapel—the spires of the cathedral have never been finished—to the Italian stonecutters. Their work of stonecutting was precise and balanced, always alike on both sides. So, when they erected the walls of the chapel, they made opposite sides alike. If there was an opening in this wall, directly opposite must be a similar opening in the other wall. This was in the year 1878.

Having finished the walls, the roof, and the spire, they turned their attention to the interior and put up the choir loft. Then the sisters, to their dismay, found that no space had been left for a stairway leading to the choir. At that time Santa Fe had no expert artisans. The sisters consulted one native carpenter after another, but no one knew how to build a staircase to fit the space and to suit the requirements, without masking doors or windows.

"What shall we do?" asked Sister Rita, in charge

of teaching the young ladies music. "We must get up to the choir loft."

"Yes, what shall we do, Mother?" asked another.

"We must pray," said Sister Blandina, who was the practical one, the backbone of the institution. She caught up the rosary hanging in the full folds of her long black skirt.

"Yes," repeated the Mother Superior, "we must make a novena to St. Joseph, the great carpenter, to ask his help in our need. We must rise an hour earlier each morning and meet here in the chapel for our prayer."

The black-hooded, black-draped figures moved away to perform their many duties until the morning. They prayed their novena. On the very morning when it was completed, the ninth day, an elderly man, with long white beard, appeared at the convent door.

"I understand," he said, "that you want a staircase built in your chapel, leading up to the choir loft. I should like to build it for you."

Then, when the Mother Superior spoke to him of costs and payment, he told her what materials he would need, but evaded any discussion of terms for his services. "You need not worry about that," he would repeat. There would be time enough to discuss that when he had finished his job satisfactorily.

This carpenter set to work to cut out pieces of

hard wood, which he fitted with dowels to make a spiral staircase. Not a nail was used. He worked quietly, unobtrusively, and, whenever a sister would come into the chapel to pray, he would slip noiselessly away until she had finished. So the Mother Superior issued an order that no one must go into the chapel after the early morning prayer, in order that the work would not be so often interrupted.

On the morning when the job was to be completed, the sisters rejoiced. Their heels went tapping sprightly along the floors of the bare corridors. They held a little conference to decide how they could best show their appreciation to the carpenter. It was agreed to give him a feast for his luncheon. In the office they set a table. Each sister went to the kitchen to prepare her favorite dish. When all was ready and the food steaming hot, they went to call him. But he was nowhere to be found. Not a single person had seen him leave the chapel; no one had seen him on the convent grounds; no one had seen him on the streets of the little village of Santa Fe, or upon the roads leading away.

Then the sisters knew that it was St. Joseph himself who had come to build the stairway in answer to their prayers. No one else could have built so perfectly. Even today, after more than seventy-five years in a dry climate where wood warps and crackles, there is never a creak as one climbs the stairway, so well were the steps put together. The bell peels forth high above this staircase, telling its story.

Another of the newer churches, one that dates back only to 1814, is the shrine at Chimayo, in one of the valleys of the tiny *rios* cutting the Sangre de Cristo mountains. ("The Blood of Christ" mountains, because at sunset they reflect a maroon alpine glow like bright blood.) This is sometimes called the Lourdes of America because of the miraculous cures that have been effected there. As an evidence there are discarded crutches hanging on its mud walls.

The Shrine at Chimayo

THE story is told, by its bell, that in the early part of the nineteenth century, Don Bernardo Abeyta became very ill. He lived at Chimayo, a man prominent in his community, owning many sheep and many acres of land along the little river of the Holy Cross (*Rio de Santa Cruz*). As there was no hope for Don Bernardo's recovery, his family went about in tears. Their neighbors whispered condolences, the women coming always with the black shawl of mourning as a covering over their heads.

One day his daughter bundled him in soft Chimayo blankets, which had been woven by his grandmother in that very house. They set him outside on the porch in the warm sunshine that it might give him strength. As he sat there, watching the water run along his "mother ditch" on its way to water his fields and saw his flock of sheep on a nearby hillside, Don Bernardo thought of his many blessings and of the good he might do in the world if he could be spared.

When these noble thoughts came to him, Don Bernardo suddenly saw his patron saint, San Es-

The Santuario of Chimayo

quipula, standing on the opposite side of the ditch beckoning to him. Throwing aside his blankets, he arose and hobbled feebly toward the saint; but before he could get across the ditch, the apparition had disappeared. Don Bernardo went and fell upon his knees at the spot where his patron had stood. Immediately he was made well.

News of his miraculous healing spread through the countryside. All the sick were brought to the spot. Each was at once cured. To commemorate this greatest of all blessings to him, Don Bernardo built an adobe chapel, enshrining the sacred spot in a room beside the altar.

Pilgrims began to arrive, even from as far as Old Mexico. Whole families would come bringing their sick, or one member would arrive to get a bit of the curative soil for someone too ill to be brought. In the stagelike coaches of that day, gentlemen in tight leather breeches, with silken coats and striped silk sashes, would drive up with coachman and outriders. Gallantly they would alight to assist their ladies, in velvets and satins. Others would wend a slow way in creaking ox-carts, the men in big straw hats and cotton trousers, the women with calico or black merino shawls worn as hoods. Some dashed up on horseback, with their lathered steeds champing bits of silver-studded bridles and weighted beneath silver-mounted saddles, as the embroidered boots and silken garments of their riders glittered in the sunshine. Still others, in ragged cotton clothing, kicked their heels into saddleless burros, as they rode these little beasts in jog-trot to the shrine. From the highest to the lowliest, they have journeyed far for a spoonful of this miraculous soil. With all alike, it has been shared in small, precious doses, no matter whether the thank-offering left behind is large or small.

Today, where St. Esquipula stood, there is a hole about six feet deep and three to five feet in diameter, surrounded by the remains of myriad burned candles and a strange assortment of candlesticks.

In a niche on the left wall of the nave of the shrine stands a carved image of San José, holding his rod flowering with tissue paper flowers. It is an ancient statue carved from pine and colored with blanket vegetable dyes. Instead of wearing carved shoes, this San José always appears in a tiny pair of leather shoes.

Every so often this San José takes on mortal form and makes journeys during the night, far and wide over the countryside, going about in the dark on deeds of mercy. Upon such nights, he travels so fast and so far that he completely wears out a pair of shoes. Anyone wishing an especial blessing will then make or buy for the little image a new pair.

The family living next to Don Bernardo, jealous

of all the revenue his family were taking in from the thank offerings to San Esquipula and San José, built a family chapel and placed in it an almost life-sized carved image of the *Santo Niño,* the Holy Child. They, too, proclaimed that the Santo Niño wore out His little shoes on pilgrimages. Today He receives more shoes and more contributions than does the image of San José, though pilgrims still go to the shrine for teaspoonfuls of its sacred soil.

Next to Chimayo and also along the little Santa Cruz river is the village of Santa Cruz, in which the largest church in New Mexico, built in 1733, stands upon the ruins of the original chapel, which was erected in 1695. It is dedicated to Our Lady of Carmel. One arm of the transept leads into a chapel of St. Francis, and the other into one dedicated to Our Lady of Carmel. For many years a carved image of St. Francis, showing him greatly emaciated, stood in the former chapel. It had lost both hands. One hand, said the sacristan, was broken off at the time of a terrible storm, when the river rose into a tor-rential current, destroying crops, inundating adobe house walls, and doing all sorts of damage. St. Francis' hand was thrown out into the raging ele-ments, which at once became quiet. The river subsided immediately.

At another time, there was an epidemic of sick-ness in the village, taking heavy toll of the babies, as well as of older people. This was just before the beginning of Lent. The other hand of St. Francis was broken off and burned to ashes, which were then placed upon the foreheads of everyone on Ash Wednesday. After that not a case of sickness occurred.

An amusing and pertinent story is told of an old image of Our Lady of Carmel in this same Santa Cruz church.

The Image of Our Lady of Carmel

THE little carved image of Our Lady of Carmel had become somewhat cracked and mutilated during her centuries of service to the people of Santa Cruz, standing faithfully in her small niche. She was called by all the people, *La Madrecita,* The Little Mother. She had cured sick babies, soothed the hearts of deserted sweethearts, brought back straying husbands, and even healed sick lambs and burros.

There moved to a ranch not far away an American family from the east, or perhaps from California. The man, with his wife and his wife's mother, was much interested in remodeling the old ranch house and furnishing it to make it convenient, yet to keep it harmonious with the spirit and feeling of the country.

One day these people went into the Santa Cruz church to look around at its interesting old architecture and old paintings. Upon seeing the tiny image of Our Lady of Carmel, the woman became most enthusiastic.

"Look at this poor little old image, John," she

exclaimed to her husband. "She is so worn and pathetic, but isn't she a dear? Don't you think these people would much rather have a new image? Let's send for one to surprise them."

The new image was sent for. It arrived in all its fresh color, its gilt trimmings and splendor. The couple slipped down to the church that evening after dark. Taking out the little old image, they replaced it with this resplendent new one. They took the old carved *santo* home with them and placed her in the niche in their living room, where she "just fitted exactly."

"Won't the people be pleased when they find what we have done for them?" asked the wife, trying to deceive herself.

At dusk the next evening, the newcomers heard chanting coming down the roadway toward their ranch house. Going out on the porch, they saw a procession wending its way in their direction. It turned in at their gate. In its midst was a young girl dressed as for first Communion, fresh-looking and beautiful, with soft brown hair, wavy beneath the white net veil, smooth olive skin, large eyes, soft and brown, and regular features. Most of the time she kept her eyelids down in modesty, and in her firm brown hands she carried a prayer book of white leather, embossed with gilt.

Finally the group stopped in front of the porch.

The young girl was led forward by a spokesman.

"We have brought you a new mother," he said, assuming great deference. "Your mother she is old. She is wrinkled and ugly. We feel sorry, so we bring to you a new mother. This one, she is young. She is very pretty. She has one pretty white dress. You will love her. We bring her. You take her and you give to us your old mother you do not want." He led the girl up the steps and reached for the mother.

For a moment the woman on the porch stood with mouth wide open in astonishment. Then quickly she turned and went inside. When she came out again, without a word, she handed to the spokesman the image of Our Lady of Carmel, The Little Mother.

You may see her in the church today.

It is also said that the bell of the Santa Cruz church rings out a story similar to that of the bell of San Miguel. It is the tale of a tragic betrothal.

The Tragic Betrothal

WHEN the news of the colonization of Nuevo Mejico reached a certain small town in Spain, with exaggerated tales of rich veins of gold and silver ore, a young man, Don Angelo, resolved to cross the ocean to this new land to win his fortune.

Shortly before, he had been betrothed to the most beautiful young señorita of his village, Doña Teresa. For her he wanted all the luxuries of the Spain in that day of its "Golden Age." He must have a fortune so as to give her all that she might desire, all that she ought to have to set off such beauty. Don Angelo decided he would go to this New Spain, establish himself there, and then return to Spain to get his bride and bring her to the new home.

The whole village, when they heard of his plans, held *fiesta* to bid him Godspeed. There was dancing day and night along the narrow streets and in the decorated plaza. There were processions with colored paper figures and paper clowns to burst and shower gifts. There was feasting, with sweetmeats and wine. The town could not settle down from such gaiety even after Don Angelo, with a last wave of his cocked hat, galloped away to his ship. As a parting gift, he gave to Doña Teresa a gold cross on a gold chain.

After months of hard travel, Don Angelo came to the newly established village of Santa Cruz. But shortly after his arrival, the hostile Apache Indians made an attack upon the settlement. In the fight, Don Angelo was killed.

Long afterward, for news traveled slowly, the village of Don Angelo heard of his death. Doña Teresa's grief was inconsolable. She would see no one. She even refused to go to church. Her father decided to have a bell cast to be sent to Santa Cruz in memory of Don Angelo, hoping that this would somewhat assuage his daughter's grief and lead her back, when she heard other church bells, to the comfort of the Mother of God and the saints.

While the bell was being cast, the whole village held a mourning for Don Angelo. Doña Teresa, with tears streaming down her cheeks, walked slowly to the molten mass of metal. Into it she threw her gold engagement ring and the gold chain and cross, which had been the parting gift of her lover. This so moved the other youths and maidens that they, too, slowly walked around the caldron throwing into it their jewels of gold and of silver.

The sweet-toned bell came to Santa Cruz and hangs in the belfry of its church. When it rings, it reminds the old-timers of the beautiful love and tragic betrothal of Don Angelo and Doña Teresa. Often it rings of its own accord on the anniversary of Don Angelo's death.

Santa Cruz de Cañada (Holy Cross of the Little Canyon), as the village is properly called, was settled shortly after La Villa Real de la Santa Fé de San Francisco de Asis (The Royal Village of the Holy Faith of St. Francis of Assisi), which is now called simply Sante Fe. Another of the early settlements was the town of Tomé. In fact, the first post office in New Mexico was at Tomé. Its name is a contraction of Abbé Santo Tomas. But the name by which it was always known among the Comanche Indians was The Town of the Broken Promise.

The Town of the Broken Promise

IN THE middle of the eighteenth century, Don Ignacio Baca came from Spain at the head of fifty families. Having a grant of land from the Spanish Crown, they settled the town of Santo Tomas, which they fortified with a high mud wall against the hostile Indians all about them. As the Comanches were most to be dreaded at that time, Don Ignacio set about establishing friendly relations with them. Sending a special delegation to them, he invited them to come into Tomé to trade.

The Comanches accepted the invitation, coming at the same time each year for trading. During these visits the Spaniards always received them cordially. At length between the chief, who was a tall, intelligent man, and Don Ignacio, a close friendship sprang up.

One year this chief brought with him his ten-year-old son. He and Maria, the little daughter of Don Ignacio, took a fancy to each other and began playing together. Maria also attracted the attention of the Comanche chief.

"Our children like each other," he said to Don

Ignacio. "Let them be married to each other when they are grown up. Then Comanches and the people of Tomé will always be brothers; never any more troubles between them."

"That is good," replied Don Ignacio. In a council meeting, the promise was sealed in a solemn compact, followed by an elaborate feast of barbecued lambs and other favorite dishes, the best that the town could supply. After this, in high spirits, the Comanches returned home.

Each year thereafter, when the Comanches came to trade, the chief brought handsome gifts of horses, buffalo robes, beads, and baskets to little Maria.

At last, when the Indian lad was nineteen, the whole Comanche tribe rode their finest horses to accompany the young man to Tomé for the wedding. For weeks before, their squaws had been busy chewing skins soft, beading them, wrapping eagle feathers for new war-bonnets, staining and fringing buckskin leggings, and making new fringed buckskin dresses for themselves, with porcupine quills and beads in elaborate designs upon them. Decked in all this fresh finery they came, this time with gifts of buffalo hides, buffalo tongues, beaded vests and moccasins for Don Ignacio and his wife. It was a gay cavalcade, dashing up with whoops of pleasure.

Weeping copiously, Don Ignacio met them. He

said to the chief: "Maria died last winter with small-pox. It has taken my heart away. I fear that I, too, shall die." He wiped his eyes and blew his nose.

The Comanche chief and his followers expressed deep sympathy. They nodded and grunted dolefully. Leaving their gifts, they returned home in sadness to hold their dance for the dead.

When Don Ignacio had made the promise of giving little Maria in marriage to the Comanche's son, he was afraid of these warlike Indians. He would have promised them almost anything to insure peace. Since that time his settlement had increased in the number of inhabitants. The Indians had all been peaceful. Now there seemed no need to make such a sacrifice for them. He had changed his mind about marrying Maria to the Comanche's son. After all, a promise made to an Indian "did not count."

So, when Don Ignacio discovered that the Comanches were on their way to celebrate the wedding, he arranged with the people of the town to keep Maria in hiding during the stay of the Indians. Then he pretended that she was dead.

All went well for a year. Then, as always happens, the deception was betrayed. The nearest settlement to Tomé was the Indian pueblo of Isleta. There was constant intercourse between the two places. With a pack train of burros, a party of

Isletans went over to trade in the Comanche country. During the trading, the Comanche chief mentioned the sad death of Maria Baca. The Isleta Indian looked up in quick surprise.

"Maria is not dead," he exclaimed. "I saw her at Tomé just a week ago when I took pots to trade for chili peppers."

"Yes, I saw her, too, not a month ago," said another from Isleta. They had all at some time during the past year seen Maria.

The Comanche chief, incensed over the trick, immediately started to plan revenge.

The people of Tomé, being ignorant of what the Isleta Indians had told, had no fear of the Comanches. They had long since ceased to keep lookouts watching for them and to be constantly on guard against an Indian attack. They were living their lives without any thought of Indians.

When the 8th of September arrived, which is the feast day of Santo Tomas, the patron saint of Tomé, the inhabitants went first into the adobe church to attend Mass before entering upon the grand celebration of a chicken pull, horse races, feasting, and dancing.

While Mass was being celebrated, a terrible warwhoop sounded from the outside. The congregation arose from their knees in panic. Don Ignacio sensing the cause of the trouble, hid Maria behind the altar and turned to face the enraged Indians. Hideous in war paints, they began at that moment to pour into the church. They advanced, seizing young girls and shooting or knocking down men and boys as they came. All the while, they searched for Maria. They had determined to take her away, dead or alive.

One of the Comanches gave a blood-curdling yell. He had found Maria behind the altar. As he was dragging her out by the hair, the chief raised his hand for the slaughter to cease.

The Comanches took Maria away, with many other young women and with children for slaves. In their own country they celebrated Maria's belated marriage to the son of the chief.

It is said that Maria was well treated and was very happy. She has many descendants among the Comanches, who still bear the name of Baca. The Comanches have always called Tomé, The Town of the Broken Promise.

There were a number of misunderstandings of one kind or another between Spaniards and Indians. Sometimes these were merely misinterpretations. Among tales of this sort is one which the bell of San Juan church rings out.

Santo Niño Brings the Rain

NO ONE can live long in New Mexico without hearing the story of how Santo Niño de Atoche once too thoroughly answered the prayers of the Indians. Nambé Indians say that it happened at San Ildefonso; but at San Ildefonso you will be told that it was at Tesuque; while one man from San Juan tells that it really happened at San Juan when Father Seux had charge of that parish. But wherever it took place, it is a good story.

One year a dreadful drought settled over the country, drying the young corn into rustling yellow ribbons. The Indians held their rain races, beat their drums in imitation of thunder to invite the thunder storms, shook gourd rattles sounding like the patter of raindrops to coax the showers to come, and went through all their ceremonies that in years past had brought rainfall. But these old methods completely failed, for the white man had brought in new ways with a new God and His saints. They prayed in a different way, which so confused the elements that they no longer responded to the entreaties of the Indians. Everything had gone wrong

The Mission at Santo Domingo Pueblo

since the white man came. The Indians could no
longer control the weather and bring the rains.

After exhausting their own ceremonies without
results, the Indians held a council to discuss the
situation and to find out what they could do next.
At the meeting, someone suggested that they might
appeal to the saints of the white man since everything else had failed. So they appointed a delegation of their number who could speak Spanish,
and sent them to interview the priest.

"Padre," said the leader, "we wish to have Santo
Niño to take him in procession around our corn.
The rains do not come. The corn is drying up, and
soon the Indians will have nothing to eat."

The padre took them into the mission and allowed them to carry away the image of Santo Niño
de Atoche, wearing His plumed hat and sitting
upon His little wooden chair.

That evening at twilight, little horizontal flames
flickered and smoked in the breeze as the candles
were carried, smothering then flaring, in a line
around the corn fields of the pueblo, and the soft
chanting of bits of the litany, all that the Indians
could remember, floated away on the same breezes.
In solemn procession they were taking the image
of the Christ Child around their fields as a prayer
for the rains to come to save their staple food.
Shortly after dusk, still in procession, they returned

the *Santo* to His niche within the mission and, with only half-hearted faith, went sadly home. No rain had fallen upon the procession.

But at midnight the stars were completely hidden by dark clouds, piling rapidly from all parts of the horizon. A great black mass settled over the pueblo fields, cut through by vivid flashes of zigzag lightning, causing the whole village to shake in the succeeding crashes of thunder. Suddenly the whole heavens seemed to open in a downpour of stinging raindrops, which washed away the mud walls of houses, made a pond of the sunken plaza, and sent walls of water rushing down the *acequias* and dry *arroyos*. Their prayers had been answered.

At daylight, when the Indians went out to see the results of the rainfall, they stood aghast. Their corn fields were in ruins. A multitude of washes cut across them helter-skelter like veins. The few stalks of shriveled corn to be seen were lying uprooted, half covered with soil. The rest had been entirely washed away.

Dejectedly the delegation returned to the priest.

"Padre," again said the leader, "we wish to have Santa Maria to take her in procession."

"Why do you want Santa Maria?" asked the kindly priest. "You told me yesterday that you wanted to take Santo Niño around your fields to bless them and to bring the rain to them. You took

Santo Niño and the rains came. Now why do you want the Holy Mother?"

For a moment, the spokesman stood like a statue, with head slightly drooped before the priest. Then he replied:

"We wish to take Mother Mary around our fields for her to see what a ruin her bad little boy has made."

The priest humored them in their request. They took the image of Mary around the fields, chanting as they went. The Indians will tell you today, when you look at the image of Mary as Our Lady of Sorrows, that you can still see upon her cheeks traces of the tears she shed that morning when they took her around their fields to witness the havoc of the storm.

The church bell at the Indian village of San Felipe tells a most astounding tale. History corroborates it in part, but only tradition can foster it in its entirety. History records that at the time of the Pueblo Rebellion in 1680, at Cochiti was stationed Fray Alonzo Ximenes de Cisneros. On the eve of the uprising he escaped from the Cochiti pueblo by the aid of his sacristan; but tradition would have us believe that a miracle happened to Fray Cisneros.

The Miracle of San Felipe

ON THE eve of the great rebellion, in August, 1680, the Indians of Cochiti held a council to decide how to kill their priest. When the sacristan, who was a good Christian and devoted to his priest, heard the plans, he rushed to the *convento* in the middle of the night.

"Padre, Padre," he called, until Fray Cisneros was awakened. "Padre, I am your friend. The people of the village are planning to kill you as soon as the sun is up. You must fly. I will go with you to help you."

So the sacristan carried the priest, who was a small man, across the Rio Grande upon his back. He accompanied him down the highway until they reached the spot where the town of Algodones now is. Here the sacristan left him, saying: "I must return now before I am missed, for if the Indians discover that I have been away, they will kill me, too. You must now save yourself."

It was almost daylight. The priest knew that he must hide. He looked about him and saw in the middle of the Rio Grande a little island on which cottonwoods were growing thick. Deciding that this was a good place to seek shelter, the padre crossed to the island.

On that day the Indians all left their villages in search of Spaniards. Men from San Felipe came down the highway. They also placed sentinels on the mesa tops near their village to search the country below. One of these lookouts saw a large brown object upon the island. He called to others that he had found a bear.

The Indians are more superstitious about bears than about anything else. Bears have great magic. Human witches frequently change themselves into bears, capable of doing great harm if killed or mistreated, unless the bear can be killed quickly and his heart cut out while still throbbing.

As soon as the bear was discovered, a party of the San Felipe Indians crossed to kill it. They discovered that the bear was Fray Cisneros. The hunters held council. Since Fray Cisneros had been mistaken for a bear, there was some strange magic around him. Assuredly they must not kill him. They decided to save him and to take him to their pueblo. Since Indians were everywhere patrolling the country, the priest must be disguised. They took off his brown robe and stained his body, face, and hands brown. Each Indian then contributed an article of clothing. Having thus dressed him as an Indian, they set out for San Felipe. On the way they passed a group of men from Cochiti searching for their priest.

"Have you met Fray Cisneros?" asked one from Cochiti.

"No, we have not," replied those from San Felipe. But, at that moment, one of the Cochiti men saw the friar and recognized him through his disguise. They demanded that he be turned over to them. But the friar had been mistaken for a bear. There was magic about him. The San Felipe men refused to give him up. A scuffle ensued, lasting all the way to San Felipe pueblo.

When the Indians were safely in their own village with the padre, the men of Cochiti went away to get reinforcements for a siege of the village. Next day they returned with many more from their own pueblo and with help from the pueblo of Santo Domingo.

The Indians of San Felipe, seeing how many were their foe, retreated to the top of the mesa behind their village and entrenched themselves on its high summit. For many days they were besieged until their supply of water completely gave out. The warriors called a council to discuss the situation. The padre, insisting that he was the cause of all their trouble, offered to give himself up to the enemy, so that they would go away. But, as the padre had been mistaken for a bear, they could not let him do that. Then the priest suggested that he should spend the night in prayer for spiritual guidance as to what to do on the morrow. The Indians agreed.

Searching in his wallet, the padre found a small piece of paper and, picking up a piece of charcoal from the campfire, he wrote words upon it. This he gave to the sacristan, bidding the man take it to a certain spot, put the paper down with the writing face down, and place a stone on it to keep it from blowing away.

Fray Cisneros went off by himself and prayed. At daybreak, he asked the sacristan to bring the paper. Lo, upon the other side was also writing! When the priest had read the writing, he asked for a piece of obsidian, black volcanic glass, which he chipped and sharpened to a keen edge. Then he ordered all the people to bring to him their jars and gourds. When all were assembled, he bared his arm, gashed it with the sharp glass and held out the cut over the water vessels. Immediately there poured from the wound a stream of clear water, which flowed until the last vessel was filled. For many days the enemy remained, but always when the jars were empty, they were filled with water from the priest's arm. The Indians gave thanks to God. Finally the men from Cochiti and Santo Domingo grew tired and went home.

The Indians on the mesa returned to San Felipe. Fray Cisneros remained with them for many years. For many more years the Indians celebrated with *fiesta* the "Day of the Padre," in commemoration of the great miracle.

The bells of the San Felipe mission tell of Fray Cisneros when they ring. In a little chapel at Cienega the thin slab of granite, worn where it has been struck as a bell, rings clear notes telling the story of an image of San José brought up from Mexico by another of the early priests.

San José at Cienega

AN EARLY priest, Father Joseph, came to the little pastoral community of Cienega near Santa Fe, bringing with him an image of his patron saint, San José. This image was almost life-size and beautifully carved.

In the community was one man rich in lands, in cattle, sheep, and horses. When the priest arrived, this man built for himself and his family a private chapel and invited Father Joseph, since there was no public church in the valley, to place his image within this chapel. Father Joseph did so. The wealthy man also offered to let the padre celebrate Mass in his chapel for all the people of the neighborhood, since there were few who were not retainers of this man of wealth.

Shortly after this, Father Joseph's sister, with her family, followed the priest to settle near him in Cienega. They all lived very happily until the priest grew ill. When he was dying he called his sister to his bedside and said to her: "There is nothing I have loved so much as the image of San José, who has encouraged me in times of distress, upheld me through discouragements, comforted and sustained me. Pray to him every day, my sister. Let him always help the people of Cienega. I leave him in the care of you and your descendants. Whenever there is a church built in Cienega, have him placed within it."

For some years the image of San José stayed in the rich man's chapel. When he died, his son decided to sell his possessions in Cienega, to give the family chapel to the community, and to move to Algodones on the Rio Grande. Through the deep-rutted, muddy roads of the marshy land, he transported all his movable possessions with ox-carts, their great solid wheels wabbling and creaking as they went.

At length he came back to take away the beautiful image of San José, to place it in his new family chapel at Algodones. The statue, more than five feet in height, was carefully wrapped in a striped blanket and placed upon the ox-cart, drawn by two oxen. As the oxen plodded along, their load grew heavier and heavier. They began to sweat, to breathe heavily; they had to be goaded, yelled at, and urged in every way to keep pulling. At length, several miles from the chapel, they stopped. Their tongues hung out. They were drenched with sweat. Their deep breathing could be heard for a distance.

Their sides heaved. The drivers whipped and yelled. The oxen strained and then fell dead.

Astounded at such a mishap, the peons returned to report the disaster to their patron and to get fresh oxen. This time they brought an extra yoke and four of their heaviest beasts. These were hitched to the cart bearing the image of San José and urged to go forward. The oxen tried to take a step forward, but the cart did not move. The yoke creaked and the animals were jerked back. Once more, at the lash of the driver, they strained forward. Muscles showed in great cords along their necks and in their sinewy legs. The cart would not move. Again and again the driver lashed them. Again and again they strained, until they, too, were drenched with sweat and heaving in exhaustion. They also fell dead.

Some people, hearing of the catastrophe, gathered at the scene. One of them asked: "What are they hauling that is so heavy?" The answer came: "The image of San José."

"But that belongs to the people of Cienega, to the family of Father Joseph. I shall go and tell them," said the first speaker.

Off he rode at a gallop to tell the nieces and nephews of the late Father Joseph. Hastily two of the men grabbed up the narrow cot from their front room. Down the road they ran with it, directed by the man on horseback. When they reached the ox-cart, the drivers had gone to get six fresh oxen for their cart. Father Joseph's nephews reached over and lifted the image, now having only the weight of light wood. They placed him on their cot and went chanting along the road to return him to his regular niche in the chapel. There you can see him today.

When the drivers returned with their oxen, they hitched the first pair to the yoke of the cart. Before they could hitch the others, these two, who were young oxen, became frightened and began running down the road with the cart. Its great axle shrieked as they ran. With surprise, the drivers looked at each other. They caught the run-aways; but, looking into the cart, they found that the image had gone, and they knew that San José had purposely made himself too heavy to be carted away, because he belonged to the people of Cienega. He wished to stay there to give the people his blessing. And when the old stone slab, once used as a tom-tom by Indians, and later used to call the people of Cienega to church, is struck, it rings out this story of San José.

There was another man of wealth in the Chama valley, near the Indian village of Abiquiui, which was fast becoming mixed with Spanish blood and, therefore, more Spanish than Indian in customs.

It was a favorite place for the Navajo Indians to attack. Also there were many bandits in that country, for it was and is an especially fertile valley.

If the little church, near Abiquiui, had not been partially destroyed at the time of this tale and left as a ruin until today, its bell would be sure to ring out the following story.

The Hidden Treasure

NOW this rich don, near Abiquiui, had hoarded much gold and silver. His great iron-bound chest was full of coins. The only person to whom he ever gave money was to the priest, because he was afraid not to have the priest's blessing. He was even stingy with his only son. In his fear that his treasure might be stolen, he guarded it with great care and kept the chest in a small windowless room of the house, always with its huge hand-wrought iron padlock locked with its tremendous key. The key was always on a chain next to his body.

The Navajo Indians, when they raided, came especially for food, the fruits of the fields, sheep and goats, for horses to ride, and for women and children for slaves; but at length they learned the value of gold and silver and would take that, too, whenever it was found.

This wealthy don was aroused one day by a fast-galloping horseman. The rider drew up before the don's door and called out: "Get your gun and come into the village. The Navajos are coming on a raid." He dashed away with his warning to others.

For a few moments, the don ran back and forth in his long front room, like a frightened hen. He called loudly for his son. He called loudly for his foreman, in whom he had confidence. His call was so alarming that both men ran hurriedly to see what could be the matter.

"Come quickly. Hitch the horses to the coach, Ramon. We must take my treasure chest to the padre." When the man, Ramon, brought the horses hitched to the coach, the three men with difficulty lifted the treasure into the carriage and off they went to the church.

"Father, Father," called the don excitedly. The priest ran out. "Father, the Navajos are coming. Please let me bury my treasure beneath the altar of the church, where St. Francis will keep it safely for me."

"But, my son," said the Father hesitantly. He could not finish his sentence, for the don interrupted.

"Here, Father, help us. It is heavy to lift."

The don had been kind and generous to him, so the padre helped lift the chest and drag it into the church. Swiftly the men dug a hole directly beneath the altar. Into it they placed the chest. When they began to throw dirt upon it, the don cried out: "Place a curse upon anyone who disturbs this chest, padre."

The priest quietly answered: "No, that would be a sin, my son; but we shall ask a blessing only upon the owners of this treasure. May it bless only its owner, our don here, and his son."

For a long time no sound was heard but the crunch and thud of earth, followed by the slap of spade packing down the surface. Then suddenly a war-whoop rent the stillness. In a moment the Church was filled with nomadic Indians, their long black hair framing faces ornamented with decorations in bright paints, their brown bodies bare and glistening, their buckskin leggings and moccasins soiled from long, fast traveling.

The Spaniards were helpless, having only their picks and spades with which to fight. The Indians shot them down and dragged them into a pile. Ramon, who had gone to look after the horses, alone escaped. The Indians set fire to the woodwork of the doorway and went on to the town. The church was only partially destroyed, since its thick mud walls could not burn, and the flames could not travel far; but it was damaged beyond use until it should be repaired. After the raid, the impoverished people were too busy trying to find enough food to think of the church. When they did finally turn their attention to it, they decided to leave the church as it was and to build a new one within the village.

Bandits learned that the late don had possessed great treasure. They also heard that he had had a trusted servant, Ramon. They found Ramon late one night.

"Tell us where the don's treasure is," they demanded.

Ramon shook his head, but they began to twist his hands and arms until he cried out in pain: "It is buried." For a long time they tortured him, until poor Ramon was forced to lead them to the church ruins and point to the spot at the altar where the treasure had been buried.

One of the bandits, taking a spade, walked to the spot and began to dig. When he lifted the first spadeful of dirt, with a gasp he fell dead. The eyes of the others, who were following to help with the digging, opened wide with fear. Dropping their spades where they stood, they rushed to the dead man, lifted him, carried him out, and hastily fastened him to the back of his horse. Then, leading the horse, they galloped away, never once looking back.

In awe, Ramon told this story to his friends. The bruises and marks of abuse upon his arms and body confirmed his tale. The treasure was a curse to all but its former owners, who were dead. No one has ever dared to dig for it since. According to old-timers, the treasure chest, filled with its coins of gold and silver, still lies buried beneath the altar of the ruins of the old church, whose bell has so long been silent.

Perhaps the strangest of all the stories ringing out by the bells of the missions of the Southwest are the legends of Maria Coronel.

The Visits of Maria Coronel

IN THE year 1602, at Agreda in Castile, Spain, a daughter was born into a family of nobility. She was christened Maria Coronel. As she grew up, her unusual physical beauty brought many suitors for her hand, but Maria would have none of them. She was too interested in her studies, in which she showed rare intellectual gifts, and in her determination to lead a religious life.

"I cannot understand these strange dreams of Maria's," her mother would say with a sigh. "She thinks she has some special mission to perform and she is determined to enter an order devoted to the uplift and education of the poor."

Maria succeeded in entering the religious order in her town. She began to write religious books, which were later widely used, and she also kept a detailed diary. The poor learned to love this nun in her blue habit, and she became intensely interested in the need of missionary work to be done among the Indians of the New World.

As she grew older, her religious meditations became more and more intense, so that she would fall into trances, lasting for hours, which caused grave concern among the other nuns.

"She's been lying there like that for hours, Mother," whispered Sister Angelica, with suppressed concern. The two nuns stood in the door of a tiny cell, cold in its whiteness and simplicity. On the hard cot, fully dressed, even to bonnet, wimple, and circlet, lay Sister Maria Coronel; her eyes closed tight, with blue veins showing through their pallor, and with cheeks blanched. Upon her breast she held a rosary in folded hands.

"Another of her strange visions about America," replied the Mother Superior, slowly shaking her bonnet, as she shook her head.

"But she must see something, Mother," replied the sister, in defense. "She tells about them so vividly that I feel I can see the Indians myself. She calls their names; tells how they live and what they eat and everything about them."

Sister Maria Coronel stirred slightly upon her cot. The Mother Superior hastened away so that the waking sister might not know she had been watching. Sister Angelica went in and stood at the foot of the cot, as Maria's eyes slowly opened. At first they seemed lifeless, with a strange blankness; then they blinked once slowly, opening with their usual intelligent expression.

"Oh, Sister," she exclaimed to Angelica, "I've

been on another pilgrimage among the Indians of
America. They are in such need. I feel very tired.
Please hand me my diary quickly, so that I may
write down what I have seen and done, before it
is forgotten."

"Where did you go, Sister Maria?" asked the
nun, turning to bring the diary from the low table,
upon which a group of prayer books also lay.

"I went across a long distance of arid country
northeast of Mexico, where the land was covered
with tall grasses, to visit Indians, who call themselves Tejas. Sickness was among them. The water
they were drinking was red with mud. I showed
them how to let it settle before they drank it. In
one hut there were medicine men, without clothing and with their bodies grotesquely painted, so
obscene that I had to cast down my glance in
shame. They were shaking rattles over a little sick
girl, who cringed and grew worse through fright.
When I went to where the child lay upon skins on
the cold earth and placed my hand upon her dirt-
grimed forehead, I felt it was burning with fever.
Her bright eyes, wide with panic, looked fear-
fully into mine, like a little trapped wild animal.
'Please,' I asked White Feather, their chief, 'send
these medicine men away and let me pray for this
child.' White Feather grunted and nodded at the
men, who slowly went out. One of them looked

back at me with doubt and displeasure upon his face. The child was afraid of me, too, until I spoke to her in her own dialect, which God had placed upon my tongue. I knelt there to say my beads, praying to our Blessed Mother Mary to ask God to show His power to these ignorant children by restoring the health of this little sick girl. While I was praying, beseeching the Blessed Mother to have mercy upon a child, the child fell into a deep, natural sleep and, when I had finished and placed my hand upon her forehead, it was moist and cool. Then the Indians begged me to go into the hut of each of the sick, where God was good to me and caused each to get well. They wanted to know how I had effected the cures, so I explained to them about God, the all-Father, His son Jesus the Christ, and the Blessed Mother. They begged me not to leave them, but I promised them that another teacher would soon come in my stead, who could help them even better than I. Then I left, and now I am here. I must write these things down before I forget."

Sister Angelica, who had been listening in awe, now tiptoed from the cell, leaving Sister Maria Coronel busily writing in her diary.

And so, time and time again Sister Maria Coronel lay rigid upon her cot in Agreda, Spain, while her spirit made its pilgrimages of mercy and in-

struction among the Indians of Texas, New Mexico, and northern Mexico. She died in 1665. In
her diary she kept careful records of these visits,
describing the different Indians: their habits,
clothing, and even the native names of tribes. All
of these things were afterward verified by the early
priests, who visited the same spots, though no
white man entered the territory of some of these
Indians that Maria described accurately in detail,
until years after her death. The Indians themselves later told of her visits, describing her mi-
nutely. The last of these visits was made in 1631,
for they ceased soon after the priests began their
mission work.

One day an Indian in Texas came to Fray Manzanet, according to his records. "I want some blue
cloth for my grandmother," said the Indian. "She
is sick. She will soon die. She wants some blue
cloth for a dress to be buried in, like the blue dress
that Maria Coronel wore when she came to see
my people. She came when my grandmother was a
little girl, and she took good care of our sick. My
grandmother was sick and she made her well.
Maria Coronel taught our Indians many things.
My grandmother wants to see Maria when she
dies, so she wants to wear the same kind of blue
dress." Fray Manzanet writes that he gave the Indian some blue cloth for the dress.

Scattered among the Indians, all the way from Texas to the Pacific, are legends of this strange woman, who appeared from nowhere in particular and mysteriously disappeared again. These numerous legends are in agreement in saying that the mystic visitor was of the white people, young, beautiful, and always dressed in blue; that she taught about Jesus Christ and His Mother Mary; that she proclaimed herself the herald of teachers and missionaries who would come later; and that she was held in great love and veneration by all the Indians.

Fray Alonzo Benavides was custodian of the New Mexico mission field from 1621 to 1630. During that time he made extensive reports to the King of Spain, which are compiled in his *Memoria*. In this he mentions the visits of Maria Coronel to the Indians of New Mexico during his term as custodian, though he does not record that he saw her himself.

The astonishing fact is that there is absolutely no record of Maria Coronel's ever having left Spain. It would have been impossible for a young woman of such prominence to set sail on any of the few ships setting out to the New World in those days, without someone finding out about it. So it seems conclusive that Maria never once set physical foot out of Spain. In 1631 Maria made a written confession that her visits to the Indians were made only in trances. After that year she made no more visits to them.

Yet Fray Manzanet heard of Maria Coronel from the Texas Indians in 1690; the padres of the San Agustin mission record hearing of her visits from the Indians beyond the Pecos river in 1668; Fray Benavides mentions her in New Mexico; Saint-Denis, the French adventurer, mentions in his letters between 1710 and 1714 of having heard legends of Maria Coronel among the Nacogdoches Indians; and even as late as 1775, Fray Junipero Serro makes vague reference to her visits to the Indians of California.

Did Maria come or did she not? The bells of the Indian missions say that she did.

And now comes the dearest of all the legends, one that the Christmas bells ring out.

It is believed throughout New Mexico that at dusk on Christmas Eve the Christ Child passes. He is going about to bestow His blessings upon all who are ready to receive them. He is ragged, tired, and hungry, and in search of succor. Old people have seen Him as He passed; but He has entered no house.

Every Christmas Eve at twilight, all the natives of New Mexico build bonfires in front of their houses to light the Child upon His way and to invite Him to come in if He will. These lights, by showing Him the home and showing that a blessing is expected there, bring His blessing to it. Many are the tales of these blessings and of what almost miracles have been performed while the bonfires were burning. Marta's family is an example of the simple peasant folk who know that they are blessed by the passing of the Holy Infant.

The Passing of the Christ Child

MARTA waved her hand to her mother and father who, with quick steps, were following six loaded burros down the steep path.

Her mother stopped. Pulling back from her mouth the black shawl which served as both hood and wrap, she called to her,

"Remember, Marta dearest, to keep Tito away from the fireplace. We shall be back in the early afternoon. This evening will be Christmas Eve; we shall be here before the Christ Child passes. Watch Tito, Marta my little dove," and she hurried to catch up with her husband.

Marta stood there shivering in the cold dawn, watching her parents as long as she could see them descending into the valley. The legs of the donkeys twinkled as they swayed beneath the loads of short sticks of firewood, neatly packed upon their backs. The wood was to be sold in Santa Fe to buy coffee and sugar and perhaps a gift for Marta herself.

As she turned back into the house, Marta wondered what this gift might be. She wanted a ball, one that would bounce high when she threw it on the ground; but no doubt it would be stockings— nice long, black stockings without any holes in them. After all, she might like the stockings better; they would keep her feet warm.

High above the village of mud houses on the tiny river, Marta's one-room adobe home clung tightly to the steep mountainside, like a big mud-dauber's nest. In it she lived with her parents and her toddling baby brother.

Marta had never been far away from this spot, where her father grew chili peppers and cut wood to sell in Santa Fe. Her world was bounded by the high Sangre de Cristo Mountains, towering on all sides above her, and by the winding valley below.

No farther than this valley had Marta ever been. Here she had attended Mass in the great mud mission church, the church of Ciruela. Of the great outside world beyond, she knew nothing, except as her parents brought back tales of the wonderful things they saw in Santa Fe. Marta did not quite understand these tales of immense windows behind which were baby dolls that could say "Mama."

These stories made Marta wonder and, though she marveled, she could not understand, for they did not seem real. She liked much better the tales that her mother told on long winter nights of the tricks of the coyote, who was so often outwitted by the cunning rabbit. Then Marta would clap her hands, begging for more, for had she not that very morning seen the rabbit of the story scuttle through the brush as she went to fill her bucket at the tiny stream. Many a night she had shuddered at the coyote's yap-yapping in the dark. These tales were real.

But there were two stories that Marta loved best of all. One was about St. Joseph, before whom she knelt for prayers in the mission, who wore out a pair of shoes each night as he walked about the country doing deeds of mercy. The other story was of the Passing of the Christ Child.

The little mud houses were so like the earth, that He could never see them in the twilight, unless His way were lighted with bonfires. Marta loved the flare of the bonfires twinkling to her sometimes from far down the valley. If the Christ Child failed to pass and bless a home, sickness and trouble would come to it during all the next year.

Marta longed to see the Christ Child as He went by. There were old folk who had seen Him or heard Him; but, though Marta had watched and listened, she had never been able to hear anything but the moaning of the wind. She knew, however, that He had always found her home, for there had always been three dancing fires outside to show Him the way.

To stay inside and watch Tito did not make the day go quickly for Marta. Every little while she would run to the window looking for the sun to see what time it was; but the sun never came. The day remained gray with a cold wind blowing. Every little while she would put a short stick of wood in the corner fireplace. She knew only from the number of sticks that burned away how time was also slipping by.

Tito, too, was restless. He missed his mother and seemed to sense the impatience of Marta and the dullness of the overcast day. To amuse him, Marta wrapped strips of old cloth round and round a stone, making a soft ball, which they tossed until it rolled into the fireplace and caught fire.

The game had been so hilarious while it lasted and the fire so dangerous, that Marta had not thought to look out the window. Now, as she looked, she seemed to be peering right into the wavy hair of a running angora goat, for falling snowflakes were making a dense, moving curtain outside the window. Could the Christ Child see in such a storm? Oh, she did hope that the snow would stop before evening.

"Eat, eat," Tito called fretfully, as she gazed into the white sheet.

"Yes, Tito, it is time to eat. We shall eat now. Come, sit down, brother mine."

But Tito would not sit down. Still muttering, "Eat, eat," he followed Marta as she poured the mutton stew, red with chili pepper sauce, into an earthen bowl. Marta sat down on the floor, Tito crouching beside her, and together they dipped little pieces of *tortilla* into the bowl of stew.

Soon Tito's head fell forward in sleep. Marta spread a blanket before the fire and laid him on it. After washing out the bowl and spoons, she went back to the window to watch.

Thicker and faster fell the snow. After a time Marta knew that it was growing late; there was a steady darkening. What had happened to her mother and father? Why had they not come back? They had never stayed so long before. What if they did not get back in time to build the bonfires, and the Christ Child should lose His way, or could not find their home? Having taken to Santa Fe all the wood that had been stacked beside the house, her father had intended gathering more for the bonfires when he returned.

Her own little fire needed another stick of wood. No, decided Marta, she would not burn any more, for there were just enough dry sticks to burn for the Christ Child. She and Tito did not really need the fire. If she kept the house tightly closed, it would remain warm for a long time. She could wrap Tito in his blanket that he slept in. The wood must be kept to light the path of the Christ Child.

Tito awoke drowsy and unhappy, and started to cry. Marta took him to the window to watch the snow, which had slackened somewhat. They could see bushes drooping heavily with their burden of whiteness, like angel trees glistening in heaven.

"Look, Tito! See the pretty trees! See, Tito, they are all dressed up for the Christ Child."

But Tito whined: "I want Mama."

Marta wanted Mama, too. Where was her mother? She had never stayed so late before. It was getting dark. Without the brightness of the fire, the house was growing shadowy and dismal. Tito, not liking the darkness, became more fretful.

The snow had ceased, and Marta could see a part of the way into the darkening valley; but no mother and father were coming. Only the darkness was creeping up slowly from far below. The bottom of the valley was already covered with a blackness that was slowly unrolling itself toward Marta's hilltop. Then, one by one, flames of fire leapt into this darkness.

"Bonfires for the Christ Child," whispered Marta.

She must build and light their bonfires, or He would not pass her way. He might even get lost in the mountains and perish in the snow, as people had done before. She must hurry. It was late; the number of fires in the valley was each moment increasing. The Christ Child would give all His blessings to those below.

She gathered up an armful of wood. Tito followed her closely, dragging his long blanket. Tito must not go outside, but he would cry if she left him. What could she do? Marta stopped to think. Then, dropping the wood with a clatter on the mud floor, she ran to a wall cupboard. Climbing to the lowest shelf, she reached up and thrust her hand into a jar upon the top one.

"Here, Tito," she called. "Here are biscuits for you. Marta will give you these biscuits if you will not cry while she goes outside. Will you be a good boy and not cry if I give you the biscuits?"

Tito agreed and, seating himself with a thud upon the floor, he held out his hands for the cookies.

As Marta restacked the wood upon her arm, she whispered to herself, "Mama will not care when she knows why I took the Christmas biscuits."

Out through the deep snow she staggered with

one armful of wood after another, building in a row, in front of the house, three latticed stacks like tall pigpens.

Suddenly she realized that she had no way of lighting the bonfires, for she had let the fire in the house die out. Below her, like a long procession in the night, flared the bonfires of her neighbors, who would receive all the blessings.

Shivering from the cold and distressed over her discovery, Marta went into the darkened house to think. Tito, still busy with his cookies, paid no attention to her as she sat close beside him, in need of comfort.

Then a thought came to her: the sudden memory of her grandfather's firesticks. She had seen her father twirl them to show how fires were started long ago. These firesticks were in the chest, and with them she could light the bonfires.

But the firesticks were not so easy to twirl as Marta had thought. Again and again she tried, only to have them slip out of her hands and fall in a tumble. Marta grew desperate. Her eyes smarted while her chin trembled. The fires must be lighted. Once more she set up the sticks over some dried moss that her mother was keeping for stuffing a cushion. Gritting her teeth, she whispered: "They must turn." She was now bearing down with all her weight. They turned.

"Oh, oh!" cried Tito, clapping his hands over the lovely sparks Marta had made for him.

Dropping the sticks with a clatter and bending quickly, Marta blew the sparks into a tiny flame, with which she lighted a pine splinter. Rushing out, she brought in a stick of wood from one of the piles, a stick with much pitch in it, and set it afire. With the stick burning like a sooty torch, she hastened from one pile to another, setting the bonfires ablaze.

A frightened scream came to her from the house. Holding her breath and clenching her fists in alarm because of the lighted splinter she had left, Marta ran in. She found the baby pointing his chubby hand toward the glare at the window, his eyes stretched wide with panic. The relief was so great that Marta's knees gave way under her. With her hand pressed against her chest, she sank down beside Tito, who continued his screaming.

"Oh, Tito, that will not hurt you. It is the light of the bonfires for the Christ Child. Come see." Lifting him to his feet, Marta led him to the window, where she, too, wanted to be.

"Pretty, pretty, pretty," cried Tito, a smile hastening the course of the last tear-drops down his brown cheeks.

Minute after minute, as the fires flared higher and brighter, the children stood there watching.

Then, as the flames began to grow smaller, Marta shivered and realized that the house was growing cold. She knew, too, that as soon as the bonfires died out, she might not be able to get another spark from the firesticks, since there was no more moss, and there would be no way to rebuild a fire.

"Tito, are you cold?" she asked, merely thinking aloud.

"Cold," repeated Tito. But when she felt his hands, they were warm. Marta wrapped him in another blanket, tying both securely around him.

"Be a good boy. Stay here and watch the bonfires, while I go to find more wood that Papa has cut," said Marta.

"I want Mama," replied Tito.

"Mama is coming," Marta said. But was Mama coming? Where was she? Marta brushed away the tears that had sprung into her eyes. Tito must not see her crying or he, too, would cry. "Look at the pretty fires, Tito." Tito looked, and Marta slipped out to light the candle in the fancy tin lantern her father had made.

Time and time again, the wind blew out the flame before she could shut the tiny tin door. With the lighted lantern, she set out upward through the snow. The path was so deeply covered that the only way she could find her course was by following the opening between the whitened bushes; and since each step caused her to sink deep, her progress was slow.

It seemed a long time to Marta before she found a clump of whiteness that she knew was a pile of wood. Gathering up as many sticks as she could carry on one arm, she staggered back, swinging the lantern in the other hand. Even with the lantern, she might have lost her direction, had it not been for the dying bonfires that still cast a faint glow from their ruddy coals. Her feet were icy, her fingers bent stiff, and her thin little shoulders ached, but she struggled on toward the three shining eyes of the night.

As Marta at last neared the house, she heard a voice calling from the valley. So faint, so far-off and tired it sounded that, had it not been calling her name, Marta probably would not have heard it. Pausing, she turned her ear forward and listened:

"Marta," it called again. It was her mother.

Dropping the wood, Marta did not notice that it struck her toes. She went leaping like a rabbit through the drifts in the direction of the call, the candlelight in the lantern almost sputtering out in the sweeping semicircle of her waving arm.

"Marta, dearest of my heart," came the call again, "are you all right? Is Tito all right?"

But before Marta could answer, she had reached

her mother's side and had slipped her free arm about her. "We were lost in the storm," the mother continued. With her husband trudging behind them, she stopped a moment to rest, her black shawl-hood flaked with snow and heavy with wetness, and her long black skirt clinging soddenly around her feet. She leaned heavily upon Marta's shoulders. Then with panting breath, she added, "We would have perished in the snow if the bonfires to the Christ Child had not guided us home."

The Church bells often tell tales of the saints and their images. These images have special duties: Santa Rita is *Abogada de los Imposibles,* she must bring to pass the impossible thing; St. Anthony must always find what is lost, especially straying sheep; San Isidro takes care of the farmer and his fields, bringing a rich harvest; Santo Niño de Atoche has charge of miners and must keep them safe; St. Ann looks after children; while St. Joseph must bring a young woman a husband. When prayers said before these respective images are properly answered, the saint must be rewarded; but if no answer is granted to prayers that have been said with true faith and reverence, the images are punished. Their faces are often turned to the wall. They are taken from their niches. They may be buried under a heavy weight of things in the bottom of a chest for a definite period, or even sealed up in their niches, by having the niches plastered over.

We shall tell the story of Basilisa and the image of St. Joseph.

Basilisa's Novena

BASILISA was in disgrace: twenty-two years old next week and not married yet.

She hurried in advance of the others from the adobe mission, where she had just attended the marriage ceremony of Anita, her younger sister. She rushed to the dusty roadway, winding with the *Acequia madre,* the mother ditch, along the shut-in valley of the Sangre de Cristo Mountains. The sunny peacefulness of the scene irritated her. It was so out of harmony with the tumult within her. And when the quiet was suddenly broken by the scrape of fiddle strings, leading the wedding procession behind her with gay little jiggy tunes, her resentment made her grit her teeth and set the corners of her mouth in a hard line.

Also flaunting her with ironic gayety, were the masses of purple Michaelmas daisies here and there, bordering the wagon road, their color intensified by the yellow daisies, like flecks of sunshine dabbing purple shadows, all blossoming as if on purpose to adorn the wedding path; the wedding path of another, one younger than herself.

Ranchos de Taos Mission

Basilisa switched her satin skirt as she tried to look with indifference upon the high peaks to which the rolling hills and the valley climbed and where the highest stand of aspens cut a yellow streak of glory. Their brilliance only mocked her. Behind those peaks was another great outside world. But what cared Basilisa about anything that lay beyond? She was no part of that. What did concern her day and night, shutting out all else, was the awful fear that she seemed doomed to remain an old maid.

At length she reached the cluster of flat adobe roofs beneath the three gnarled cottonwoods, the homes of her father and her married brothers. Since she was to help prepare the wedding breakfast, no one would think it strange that she had hurried on ahead of them all.

So many times during her twenty-two years had she crossed the hewn log spanning the *acequia,* that she did not need to watch her step. From this vantage point she looked back over her shoulder for the first time at the procession, to which she should have belonged if the rebellion within her had permitted.

At first, with the musicians masking the bride and groom, she could see only the scattered family groups behind. Women, hooded with black shawls, dragging by the hand children limping in out-

grown or stiff new shoes, with hats and bonnets
slipped awry, came briskly, sweeping up with their
trailing black skirts little clouds of dust, which
the men fanned from their faces with limp felt
hats. Young men and women in their brilliant best
trailed between, smiling at each other in a way that
made Basilisa's heart miss a beat and press pain-
fully against her chest. She knew that many of
them were talking of her.

"Basilisa, she got left."

"Yes, she is already an old maid."

Or, perhaps, what was harder to bear: "Basilisa,
she too loved that Tomas."

Then, with a turn in the road, she saw the bride
and groom. Tomas, with his bright blue trousers
flaring and flapping about his heels and his collar
open at the throat, showing his thick, strong neck,
came swaying along with reckless, possessive look
in his eyes. Anita, flushed with happiness, was
glancing coyly at him from the folds of her bridal
veil. Her bouquet of bought asparagus ferns had
fastened upon it paper dollars for flowers, each
tied in the center, like alighted green butterflies.
This she held stiffly before her, the symbol of her
good fortune.

The view was too much for Basilisa. As she
turned hastily away to run into the house, a sudden tightening gripped her throat muscles.

Why couldn't she have been married before
Anita? Why had not Tomas chosen her? He was
even older than Basilisa herself and he needed
someone to cook for him and his blanket weav-
ers. Anita could not cook. Basilisa's shoulders
shrugged; but it was accompanied by an ache in
her heart. She was not so pretty as Anita, but she
could string the chili peppers twice as fast and
her tortillas were baked rounder, quicker, and
browner. But men care only for something pretty.
Every girl could not be pretty. But useful girls
were expected to go and cook for their sisters' husbands and bathe the babies. But she would not
bathe Anita's babies. She would have babies of her
own, and a stout, handsome husband, too. San
José would see to that. For eight days now she had
said her novena to him every day. This would be
her last time. To accomplish it now, she must
hurry and say her beads before her mother should
miss her and call her to serve the guests.

The long front room was now filling with them.
Sharp laughter punctuated the liquid rumble of
Spanish as they were decorously filing in, scraping
their feet upon the hard clay floor of the porch
before entering.

Her father's voice could be heard as he said with
soft graciousness: "The doors of my house are
open to give you welcome." And as each guest re-

plied that he accepted that welcome with much pleasure, Basilisa recognized each in turn as a voice that she had heard almost daily during her whole lifetime. They irritated her because she had meant so little to them. She, who wanted to mean so much!

Her mother, too, stood greeting them with limp handshakes. At that moment she was saying, "We greet you with open arms." "Open arms!" How Basilisa longed to be greeted with open arms, masculine arms to spare her disgrace!

Basilisa had wanted to escape all this. But she had been stopped by the old woman, toothless old Juana, who had been watching the kitchen while the family were all away at the mission, and thus she was kept answering questions where she could not help overhearing snatches of conversation.

"That is a beautiful dress Tomas bought for his bride," whispered a woman, with what Basilisa thought was a tinge of envy.

"Yes, and she is a very beautiful bride," replied a man, easily recognized by his deep voice.

"But is she a good cook?" asked unfamiliar tones. Who was that? She knew everyone. Oh, that must be Tomas' cousin from another village. She had forgotten he was here; but what difference did he make? And Basilisa shrugged her shoulders at the laugh accompanying the words.

"One could tell that you have already had one wife, Señor widower," responded the other. "It is not the beautiful that you now consider, but the useful wife. Is it not so? Perhaps you are right."

"Useful?" did he say. Basilisa's heart quickened. Then suddenly, before answering the persistent old Juana, she thought: "Always they are making fun of those who can do things." Basilisa frowned. She must get away while her mother was still receiving the visitors, or she would not have time for her prayers. Whispering hurriedly that she had to go behind the house for a moment, she snatched herself away from the bony fingers grasping her arm, and old Juana, with a knowing nod, let her pass.

Basilisa sought the image of San José in her mother's bedroom, cautiously closing the door behind her. It was wrong to hurry through one's prayers, but what else could she do? Her novena must be finished and it must be done today. San José, the patron saint of the family, never failed to bring a girl a husband if she prayed to him with proper faith. Basilisa knew of many cases where it was true, and he would not now fail her, for she had lighted her candle before him and told her beads five times each day for eight days and she would finish today. Basilisa had only started her novena when she had heard of Anita's wedding date. Tomas was in such a hurry to marry. He had not given her time enough. If she had known sooner, she could have finished her prayers before the wedding. Now she might be interrupted and never finish if her mother should miss her. But then surely San José would see to that, too, surely he would not let her be interrupted.

Only one admirer had Basilisa ever had and even of that one she had not been sure. Tomas had always brought him to church to walk home with Basilisa so that he might have Anita to himself. But she had despised this Filiberto. He was pock-marked. He was even younger than herself. From the very beginning she had hated him for picking up the handkerchief which she had dropped in front of Tomas, after the Mass of Our Lady of Guadalupe. Tomas had pretended not to see it and walked off with Anita, and that Filiberto had handed her the handkerchief and walked beside her. Not a word had they said. She had nothing to tell to that Filiberto. After that, it was always Anita for Tomas, while she had been thrown with Filiberto.

Dancing in the front room had begun. Basilisa could hear the squeak of fiddle strings and the thump of the guitar scraping out a tune which was almost drowned by the scrunch of sand beneath heavy shoes on the irregular board floor.

The young men were probably smiling into the faces of their partners, whose downcast eyes might hide the joy in them, but whose lips would be tell-tale in their smiling corners. Why could not some-one be smiling into her eyes? That Filiberto was there. He might dance with her and smile at her, but she hated him. Everyone else, everyone except the widower, the cousin of Tomas, who had come from another village, she had known always. Each of them had his own girl. Each of them would have a wedding in the old adobe mission. Perhaps two couples would be married at once to save the visiting priest too many trips up the steep mountain roads. Why could not she be married today at the same time with Anita? She must pray, pray now to complete her novena before the image of San José standing in his niche beside the little corner fireplace.

Quickly she lit another candle before San José; San José in a white gown trimmed with lace, covering the pastoral robe carved of pine, holding a stiffly bent wooden Christ Child on one arm and grasping a staff with the other hand, a long staff adorned at the top with gay colored tissue paper flowers. Basilisa herself had made the flowers, for San José had always been her solace since early childhood. Many times, with tears of self-pity, she had knelt before him with the palms of her hands pressed tight together, pointing upward, and each time she had been calmed and her pain eased. Just this once more she must tell her beads five times and he would send her a husband. Remembering in time the pink satin dress and the toes of her new shoes, Basilisa pulled the long rag rug closer beneath the statue, and kneeling quickly she began to chant: "St. Joseph, our protector, make haste to send me a husband."

Hastily, for fear she might be missed and interrupted, Basilisa began to repeat her petition. Once footsteps drew near the outer door and she jumbled her words forgetting for the moment what she was saying. As she said them for the last time, she was brought suddenly back to awareness of her surroundings by the sound of Filiberto's laugh coming from the outside. She stiffened. As she rose to her feet, she snuffed out the candle with an emphatic pinch. Could it be that San José intended her to marry that pig Filiberto? Was his laugh a sign? After all these years of worship and of comfort, was San José playing a trick on her? Anger flashed from her black eyes as she looked at the image of her saint, the patron of husbands, her saint who would trick her.

Basilisa stamped her foot and gritted her teeth. Her muscles twitched as she snatched up San José and, turning, swiftly threw him with all her

strength out of the window. She was still trembling
when she heard a man's voice cry out with a surprised groan, accompanied by a heavy thud upon
the hard-packed ground.

With a gasp Basilisa's hand went to her heart.
She should have known that Filiberto was outside.
His laugh had come from there. What had she
done? Had she killed him and would all the people
know of her great sacrilege and her crime? A con-
striction in her throat made it almost impossible
for her to get her breath. Suddenly her thoughts
grew more definite. She must get out of the room
and mingle with the others. Perhaps then they
would not know that it was she. They must not
know; but she must confess, she must confess right
away. Tomorrow she would get up early before
the sunrise and walk to Santa Fe to see the padre.
He would know that she did not intend to hurt
anyone. He would pray to atone for her punish-
ment to San José. But San José did need punish-
ing.

The dancers stood together as they had stopped
with the music. Filiberto was one of them. He
was standing near Basilisa, with his arm still
held around his partner, while both looked self-
consciously toward the commotion in the outer
doorway.

So it was not Filiberto. How quickly he had

come in and chosen his partner! He had known whom he wanted! Who was it? Beads of perspiration cut their way down Basilisa's whitened face. Whom had she hurt? What had she done? Through the door men stumbled against one another as they carried a limp form, while drops of blood trailed their path.

"Open the bedroom door," one of them called.

Directly toward Basilisa the feet of the bearers seemed to be staggering. Could she look up? She must know who it was. "Tomas' cousin," she whispered half-aloud.

She rushed ahead of the bearers to turn down the covers of her mother's bed for the unconscious man. When they had laid him there, Basilisa stood a moment looking down upon his face, wondering if she had killed him. He stirred and opened his eyes.

With a half smile at Basilisa, he said haltingly, "It is all right. I am not hurt much. It is only a little cut on the scalp."

And Basilisa knew from the light in his eyes, as he looked at her, that San José had brought her a husband in his own way.

So say the bells of New Mexico to the ears of her old-timers, who know all about the wonders of San José, and also of San Isidro.

San Isidro

SINCE the early inhabitants of New Mexico were chiefly ranchers, sheepmen, and miners, the most popular household saints are San Isidro, patron of farmers and protector of their fields; San Antonio, patron of flocks and finder of straying lambs and lost articles; and Santo Niño de Atoche, patron of miners and healer of the sick. Every household contains an image of one of these saints, and almost every household has its own tale of especial blessing from its particular saint, or its own idea of the saint's history and origin. San Isidro belongs particularly to Santa Fe, since he is claimed as a native. Consequently there are many tales of how and why he became a saint. One of them follows.

Isidro was a hard-working, honest rancher on a small tract of land in Agua Fria on the Rio de Santa Fe, on the outskirts of Santa Fe itself.

One year he found himself behind with his plowing. Grass was eating up his crop, and the ground was caking with dryness. So when Sunday morning came, his wife could not persuade him to go to church as usual. Instead, he hitched his two oxen to his plow and began to till his field. Neighbors chided him as they passed.

"The grass will grow and the corn will die, if you plow on Sunday," said one.

"Someday you will be plowing for the devil," suggested another.

But paying no attention to the chidings, Isidro went on with his plowing. The sunshine beat hot upon his head, and perspiration streamed into his mustachios, but he paid no heed to these discomforts.

At length, God Himself, in the form of a man, came to Isidro's field. "Why are you working on the Lord's Day?" He asked.

Without pausing, Isidro pressed his plow deeper into the stiff adobe and answered, "Because my field needs plowing right away. Otherwise my corn and beans will not grow to feed my family." With an impatient gesture, he tried to rid himself of this intruder. "It's easy to go to church, but it's hard to plow for one's family."

"This is the day for prayer," warned the Stranger. "You should be attending Mass in the church. If you desecrate the Sabbath Day, God will send rain to flood your field and destroy your crops."

"From now on I am God. Let the rains come, foolish man. They cannot harm me," boasted Isidro, wiping the sweat from his brow on a tattered sleeve.

"Then," said the Stranger, keeping pace with Isidro, "God will send a scourge of grasshoppers to eat up your crops."

"I am not afraid of grasshoppers. From now on I am God," again boasted Isidro.

"Well then, God will send a drought to dry up your beans and corn," the Stranger warned him.

"Drought cannot hurt me, for, I tell you, from now on I am God."

"Very well, then," said the Stranger; "God will send you a bad neighbor. His animals will break into your field and eat up your corn; his dog will bite you; he will gossip about you to his neighbors; and he will take away your wife. God will send a bad neighbor."

"Lord, have mercy upon me!" cried Isidro, quickly unhitching his oxen from the plow. "May God not punish me with a bad neighbor! I must go pray."

Forgetting to stall his oxen, ignoring the Stranger, and unmindful of his old clothes, Isidro ran down the road, stumbling over its ruts and stones and winding with it as the roadway traced the distinct dividing line between narrow, long ranches on the river-side and the vast green-dotted carpet of eroded land, where goats browsed, leading up to the mountains of the Blood of Christ. At last, jerking off his ragged hat, he breathlessly stumbled his way into the church, not stopping until he found his wife kneeling before the image of her favorite saint. Humbly crossing himself, he knelt beside her. Gropingly he reached for her rosary and began to recite his beads.

When the people came from church, they saw a strange sight in Isidro's field; an angel was driving Isidro's oxen and plowing his field. Thereafter Isidro became a pious and good man, so that later he was made a saint.

Today his image is shown as a hatted man, dressed in his Sunday best, walking beside an angel, who is driving two small oxen before a plow.

And this is one of the legends that the people of Santa Fe hear the bells ring out at the little church in Agua Fria.

The Fiddler Changes Heart

NOT only do the Missions have their sacred stories, but each family has some cherished legend of its own. They are often supposed to be good deeds performed by the favorite saint of the family, whose image is kept in a niche, forming a little family altar for daily prayers. One of these stories is about an old fiddler in a certain village, who played for all the fiestas, weddings, and funerals.

There was a bad sickness in the community. Babies were dying one after another almost every day. Old Juan Gonzalez had been walking slowly behind the tiny coffins, borne on the shoulders of his friends, day after day, playing on his fiddle "La Golondrina" and all the dolorous Spanish tunes, until his arms ached. At night they were so sore that he could not sleep. And so busy had he been that there was no wood in his house to keep up the fire in his little corner fireplace.

"I will not play for another baby burial," he avowed. "I don't care whose baby has died this day, I will not play for the funeral. I'm going up on top of the mesa to get a burro-load of wood."

And so Juan went outside and caught the ear of his gray burro. Taking off the hobble strap from the donkey's forelegs, he threw his coat over the beast's head and fastened on the wood-saddle. He then removed the coat and put it on himself.

"Ar-r-ray!" he cried, and the burro went trotting down the roadway, followed by Juan.

He had barely started, when a small boy came running behind him, calling loudly: "Juan, Juan, stop! Come back!"

Juan did not even turn his head. He kept on his way, as if he had not heard.

The child, still shouting as he ran, at last caught up with Juan.

"Come back, Juan!" panted the child. "Ramona's baby died last night. You must come back and play the fiddle for the funeral so that its soul may rest in peace."

"No," replied Juan, gruffly; "I will not play for the funeral. I'm going to get some wood. Go back and tell them I will never again play for a baby's funeral. Too many babies die. They can just bury babies without any music." And Juan trudged on, following his burro up the steep wagon road, leading to the top of the mesa, where piñon trees and bigger pine trees were growing.

Suddenly the burro stopped beside a huge boulder. Throwing forward his long ears, he stiffened his legs and gazed behind the rock.

"Get up! Go on!" shouted Juan. But the burro would not budge.

Picking up a stick, Juan struck the beast. "Go along, I tell you, stubborn beast!" he cried. But the burro only stiffened his legs and accepted the blows. He would not move an inch. He kept looking intently behind the great rock.

"Go on, you crazy ass! There's nothing to hurt you behind that rock," yelled Juan in exasperation. Still the burro would not move.

So Juan went forward himself to look behind the rock. Leaning there, with a short staff in His hand, Juan saw the Santo Niño Himself. Then, looking upon the ground, Juan saw the mark, which the Holy Child had drawn in the dust, the mark over which the burro could not pass.

Juan, taking off his ragged black hat, knelt in the roadway and crossed himself.

"We will go back and play for the funeral," said Juan to his donkey; and back they trudged to the village.

Grabbing up his fiddle, Juan ran to the church in time to join the procession.

Afterward, as long as Juan lived, he went about, both far and near, to play his fiddle at the funerals of all the babies. It was the wish of the Holy Child.

Mourning Doves

HERE in Agua Fria, as well as in all the valleys of northern New Mexico, turtle doves remain all the year round flying in pairs. When they are mating and cooing mournfully, all the ringing church bells will tell why they mourn.

St. Joseph was hastening with the Holy Mother and the Christ Child into Egypt to escape the fury of Herod. Walking behind the little beast, upon which Mary and Jesus were riding, he gently prodded it with his staff. The sun shone down in intense heat. The stumbling burro kicked up clouds of dust along the parched roadway, bordered by low dove weed, gray with dust and drooping with ripe seed pods. Mary kept the woolen shawl closely about herself and the Child to shut out glaring heat and stifling dust. So swathed were they that an onlooker could not tell with what the plodding burro was loaded.

A flock of doves feeding beside the road was startled. Incensed at being disturbed by a lowly burro, carrying his pack, the doves flew up into the air with a flutter, scolding loudly.

The burro shied and almost spilled his precious burden. Mary, grabbing the burro's mane, caught up the Holy Infant to her breast, and the shawl fell from her shoulders. The doves were blinded in their scolding by the brightness of the halo about the holy family and knew at once what a dreadful thing they had done. Filled with grief, they began to mourn. To this day they wear the gray cloak of repentance and mourn their deed, calling, "For . . . give! For . . . give! For . . . give!"

There are other of these little stories, many of Indian origin, telling "why" birds and animals are as they are. These stories have been given a religious significance by the Spanish New Mexicans; for these people of mixed Spanish and Indian extraction are religious-minded. They are the only real peasant group in the United States, leading simple pastoral and agricultural lives, with those deep faiths rooted in the soil. The burro is their beast of burden, the main stand-by. Naturally the mission bells can tell us why he is marked with a star upon his forehead and the shadow of the Cross upon his back.

The Sacred Markings of the Burro

ON that holy night, so long ago, when the Christ Child was born in Bethlehem and was laid in a manger, lowly animals were the first to worship Him. The glory of the Lord shone around about and the cocks crew, lambs bleated, chickens cackled, cows mooed, horses neighed, dogs barked, cats mewed, and the burros brayed. One burro was the first to bow her head, flop her ears forward, and kneel in adoration. The Lord immediately touched her forehead with a ray from the bright star shining above the manger and marked it white.

"You shall be blessed," said the Voice, "for you shall bear the blessed Savior upon all His journeys upon earth."

This was the burro on which the holy mother and the holy Infant rode on their flight into Egypt and on which Christ later rode into Jerusalem in His triumphant entry. Ever after, the descendants of this chosen burro have worn the star of Bethlehem on their brows.

When Jesus was stumbling up the hill of Calvary under the burden of His Cross, sweating blood of anguish, a lowly burro tried to wedge his way through the jeering, taunting crowd to bear the Cross in His place. He was shoved and kicked aside, while his shoulders quivered in sympathy for the Holy One. The shadow of the Cross fell upon his back and shoulders and stayed there, marked in black. Later he was caught by the soldiers and was made to bear away the timbers of the Cross. To this day, his descendants are marked by the shadow of the Cross, a black line down the back, crossed by a black line of hair over the shoulders.

Many of the inhabitants of New Mexico were simple people, struggling against the hardships of an arid land. Rain was scant and when it came it often poured in a devastating deluge, washing away crops instead of nurturing them. These people, to sustain their courage, needed a material expression, an image, of a favorite saint who had also struggled and suffered. And in their simplicity, they sometimes confused image with saint. The bells ring out many stories in which images of saints or the Christ Child have left their niches and gone forth to perform deeds of mercy. And so it happened when Juan Sena's horses were stalled.

The Stalled Horses Are Saved

JUAN SENA took off his flopping black hat and wiped the sweat from his brow with a red bandana. He peeped out from under his covered wagon and looked doubtfully at the clouding sky. A storm was coming and he was forty miles from home. He still had not sold all of his strings of chile peppers, his apples, melons, and blue corn meal. He had to buy calico yet for his wife and drive by the water mill to pick up the sack of flour on his way home. He did not want the storm to break until he had crossed that wide arroyo, where the sand was deepest and where the torrent of water raced down from the mountains. That ditch was dangerous. Many animals and many people had drowned there.

But the storm came while Juan was on his way, and the dry washes ran with turbulent floods of muddy water. As he crossed the first one, foam dashed up over the backs of his tugging horses and wet the cover of his wagon. But when he went into the biggest arroyo, the wagon wheels stuck in deep sand. The lean horses pulled and strained.

Juan urged them with lashes and yells. The water rushed faster and deeper, carrying the wagon and horses with it. The wagon swayed. It dipped into the angry current. The horses were almost torn from their footholds. Bearing his weight with all his might on the lifted side of the wagon, Juan prayed fervently to the Holy Child for help. As he felt his team, his wagon, and himself being washed away, he saw in his mind the little image of Santo Niño de Atoche which sat on its wooden chair in the niche of his bedroom.

"Santo Niño, help me!" he cried.

He felt the horses suddenly get a grip with their hoofs. The wagon righted itself. The horses gave a lunge. Swaying against the gurgling waters, the wagon was dragged up the almost perpendicular wash to safety.

As soon as Juan reached home, he went in immediately to kneel before the image of the Christ Child to pray his thanks for his rescue. As he entered the door, he found the image of the Santo Niño lying on the floor covered with mud. He knew that the image itself had come to life and had pulled him safely out of the angry waters.

El Pelon Foils the Mayor

THE mayor of the village was a hard man, a shrewd one. His political influence had come with his riches, his acquisition of lands and more lands, sheep and more sheep, until he could think of nothing but gain and power. In this longing for power he had only one foe—the priest. By kindliness the priest had won influence and support that he could not extort.

It was the eve of the patron saint's day, and all the village had been weeks preparing for it; freshly mudding outside walls, whitewashing inside walls, sweeping hard, clay courts, redressing images of the saints, buying new garments and candles and preparing for the final feast. Brass candlesticks in the mission shone, and fresh paper flowers adorned the altar. Each of the many images also enjoyed fresh tributes of paper flowers, and before each burned candles standing in their own sperm upon the clay floor, their tiny flames flickering like small licking tongues. Kneeling about them were women with starry-eyed children: older women with black shawls draped over them for hoods,

The Mission Church at Las Trampas

their lips moving in prayer; the younger women in flower-decked hats and bright colored dresses fretting over broods of restless or frightened children. Outside stood groups of men in low conversation, uncomfortable in ties and stiff tan shoes. Above them the adobe walls of the mission glowed from pulsating lights in paper sacks, lined along the wall, in which flickering candles were embedded in sand. It was still light enough for them to see rows of stacked piñon wood, like diminutive latticed towers, ready to be lighted into bonfires to border the line of march of the candle-lit procession. And beyond that tired horses stood tied to wagon and buggy wheels, and patient burros stood, some browsing with saddles on their backs, others with men's coats thrown over their heads to keep them from straying. A quiet patience filled the air as all awaited the arrival of the mayor so that the last bell might ring for Mass.

The sacristan, El Pelon the Bald One, stood with the bell rope in his hand, when at last he heard the sound of trotting hoof beats and the rasp of wheels cutting through sand. The mayor's carriage was near. At once El Pelon pulled the rope, and the bells began to chime. The knots of men grew silent. The richly dressed mayor stepped from his carriage, followed by his haughty family. As they passed into the candle-lighted church, they nodded curtly from side to side at the silent bareheaded men, who meekly followed them in.

During Mass the mayor could not keep his thoughts upon the prayers. His eyes kept wandering to the pile of wheat, corn, chile peppers in strings, and baskets of dried fruits piled high in the church corner for the subsistence of the priest. His ears were attuned only to the clink of coins falling into the collection plate.

"This priest is too popular; it's time to get rid of him," he decided. "He gets all the produce and money that should be paid in taxes to me! But I must do so without stirring up a rebellious spirit among the people." He followed the canopy, under which walked the praying priest and El Pelon devoutly carrying the image of Santo Tomas. They went round the village and between the popping, smoking, leaping flames of bonfires. But all the while he was thinking of a way to dispose of the priest. So absorbed was he that he almost singed his brown mustache with his candle flame. At last he thought of a scheme.

He waited for the priest to remove his vestments, after the ceremony, and spoke to him:

"There are doubts in my mind, Padre," he declared, "that you are a man of sufficient intellect and intuition to take proper care of this growing parish. It has greatly enlarged since you came and needs a more learned priest. I insist that you come to my house tomorrow to answer four questions that I shall put to you to prove whether you are fit for this ministry."

With this pompous speech, the bombastic mayor entered his carriage and was driven away.

El Pelon, who had been standing in the shadows and had overheard, rushed to his master.

"Let me go in your place tomorrow," he begged.

"He will know at once that you are not I," replied the troubled priest, who understood why the mayor was set upon discrediting him. He knew the questions would be trick questions that he could not answer.

"Leave all to me," replied El Pelon. "I'll make myself a wig. Have I not always been a good clown in the fiestas? Have I not always imitated everyone, so that no one knew the difference between me and the original person?"

The priest smiled and nodded.

"Then I'll go tomorrow as yourself and answer the mayor's questions. I will make them laugh." And El Pelon spent the night making his wig.

Next day when he set out for the home of the mayor, no one could have told him from the priest, not even the padre himself.

"Good-morning," greeted the confident mayor; "so you have come to answer the four questions."

The lowly would-be priest nodded.

"Answer them and I'll know that you are worthy to remain here. Fail to answer one, and you must go away tomorrow."

"I understand," mumbled the priest.

"First, answer me this: How deep is the ocean?"

"Drop into it a heavy stone. The ocean is as deep as the fall of the stone," quickly replied El Pelon.

The mayor frowned. "Then," he asked, pointing to a hill behind his house, "tell me how many sacks it would take to hold all the earth from that hill?"

"Make the sack as big as the hill and it will take only one. Make the sacks half as big as the hill, and it will require two sacks," snapped El Pelon.

The mayor was growing uneasy. "Tell me next," he demanded, "exactly how much I am worth?"

"The mayor is worth twenty-nine pieces of silver."

"Wrong," shouted the mayor with glee. "I'm worth far more than that." After a hearty laugh, he suddenly stopped and looked in puzzlement at the priest. "What do you mean by twenty-nine pieces of silver?" he asked.

"Christ was sold for thirty pieces of silver," replied El Pelon. "Your worth, worthy sir, must be only one piece less."

This answer greatly pleased the mayor. He was beginning to like this priest. Then he remembered all the grain and money the priest collected. No, he must get rid of him. His next question would fix that. "Well, fourth and last, tell me what I am thinking?" he challenged.

"You are thinking that I am the priest," quickly countered El Pelon, taking off his wig to show his bald head.

The mayor could not help laughing at the comic clown, and the ministry of the priest was saved.

This is one of the old tales brought long ago from Spain with its characters changed to suit the tongues of the mission bells, which now ring it out at Las Trampas, San Cristóbal, El Rito, Abiquiui, and almost everywhere in northern New Mexico. Some of these bells also chime forth how El Pelon once became a beggar.

El Pelon Becomes a Beggar

THE son of El Patrón, the landlord and master, upon whose vast ranch the little village was settled, had become insufferable. He had been humored and spoiled as a small child, but now that he had been away to college in Santa Fe he assumed airs of grandeur. He felt too important to associate with any of the young people of his village. It should have been a happy village, too, perched as it was on a ledge of cliff high above a fertile valley of the Sangre de Cristo mountains, like a mud-plastered bird's nest. Its expansive view should promote only noble thoughts. There was limitless distance of blue veiling. There were verdure-clad mountain peaks tumbling one behind another to snow caps. There were great red cliffs dropping sheer into sunny valleys, where clear streams wiggled laughingly.

El Pelon looked off at the view. Then he looked at the rich man's son and shook his head. In his fine clothes the boy went about looking down on the other boys, silencing their laughter, and making them feel inferior and ashamed. Something must be done about it, decided the clown, El Pelon, The Bald One. His chance came on the feast day of San Antonio, that most popular church day of the year. June was a fine month for travel, and San Antonio, as protector of the flocks, was popular with all of these mountain people who had sheep. They would be coming into the village from many miles around. He would have a large audience for himself and the son of El Patrón.

It was time for Mass. El Pelon, as sacristan, rang the first bell. Then he motioned to a lanky lad, who was watching, to come and take his place. The lad was delighted. "Ring the bell after the beggar comes," warned El Pelon.

It would take the congregation a long time to assemble. The eerie village was so filled with visitors and with horses and wagons to be encircled that they could not hurry. Even so, El Pelon knew he must make haste with his make-up.

The women and small children were already kneeling on the hard clay floor of the benchless church, each facing her particular favorite of the many images of saints on the altar, dressed in fresh silks and laces and tissue-paper flowers. No one seemed drawn to the large crucifix, conspicuously alone on the side wall. In the small hard-packed church yard, where a few sandstone grave-slabs showed that it was also the village cemetery, older men stood fanning themselves with their hats, awaiting the last bell. Boys and young men were in divided groups; beginning with the youngest around the low mud wall, shoving and punching each other with giggles or resentment, to the oldest who stood in bright blue and tan suits beside the walk to watch the girls pass by.

Against the door jamb, by himself, lolled the son of the Patrón. His fine straw hat, gaily banded, was set at a rakish angle, and in his fingers was a burning cigarette. Insolently he stared at the young women as they passed. Each of the home girls glanced at him and looked quickly away; but some of the prettiest strangers returned his nod at them with a smile.

"Look, here comes the half-witted beggar," sang out a small boy.

"Sh-sh-sh!" reprimanded his father. "It is only the simple-minded who see God."

"He hasn't been here for years," said another. "I thought he might be dead."

"He never stays anywhere more than a day," was the reply.

The little boys scampered to their parents, and the young men moved aside as the beggar came among them whining, "Alms! Alms in the name of God and San Antonio!" He moved on until he

reached the son of El Patrón. Before the lad he
knelt in supplication.

"You have fine clothes, you are rich," he cried.
"In His name give me money that I may buy myself some clothes."

Everyone was now looking at the young man
and the kneeling beggar. The lad's face grew red,
but he kept his air of nonchalance tinged with in-
solence. The church bells began to ring their last
call.

"Go in," said the boy, with a curt nod toward
the interior, "and pray. Perhaps God will give you
a new suit." He smiled, pleased with himself.

"I only asked you for alms, Señor, so that I
might ask God's blessing upon you and your gift."
The beggar went inside and knelt before the crucifix.

Men and boys crowded in to kneel where they
could, and Mass was celebrated. The Patrón's son
only shifted his position to face the altar instead
of the out-of-doors. He stood there, as the people
filed out, to once more ogle the pretty girls. The
beggar, who had been devoutly praying before the
crucifix, was the last to leave his prayers.

"Well," sneered the Patrón's son, "did Christ
give you a suit for fiesta?"

"No," replied the beggar, pointing back to the
crucifix. "My Lord is poor, as you see. He has no

clothes at all. But He made me feel rich, for I have on a shirt and trousers, you see."

Then the beggar removed his wig and bowed with ironic pomp before the young man.

"'El Pelon!'" shrieked many voices. Shouts, laughter and giggles made the son of El Patrón turn quickly and walk rapidly to his big, rambling adobe home.

And thus speak the bells of old missions in many tongues on myriad themes.

The Revelation of Cristo Rey

WHEN Don Francisco Antonio Marín del Valle was governor-general of the Territory of New Mexico in 1754–60, he built a chapel on the plaza of Santa Fe directly opposite the Palace of the Governors. He built it in the name of himself and his wife and dedicated it to Our Lady of Light. Since it was only a few hundred yards from the church of St. Francis of Assissi, his reason for the building was that the chapel might be a military chapel for the special use of soldiers. To add to its magnificence, he had a reredos carved of pinkish sandstone, weighing about thirty-five tons, so that it had to be made in many sections. It seems probable that artisans were brought up from Old Mexico for the express purpose of doing the intricate carving.

After the deaths of Don and Doña del Valle, the chapel did not flourish. By 1832 it ceased to be used. In 1855 Archbishop Lamy, the first archbishop of Santa Fe, took possession of it and had the reredos taken apart and stored in a room behind the altar of the new St. Francis Cathedral.

155

But it could still be viewed there by art lovers. The chapel was sold and razed in 1859 to make room for business buildings.

During these years many people have gazed upon this beautiful carving, 25 by 18 feet in size. They have admired the exquisite coloring of salmon-pink sandstone offset by age-softened blue paint around the figures of the saints. They have noted the Indian-like features of many of the faces and been surprised, perhaps, to find the Aztec sun symbol immediately above the panel of Our Lady of Light, Queen of Heaven, and beneath the Christ Child keystone. But no one throughout all these years saw the two aspects of the main keystone changing from the Holy Child into the agonizing Christ, wearing His crown of thorns in atonement for the sins of the world.

In 1940 Archbishop Gerkin of Santa Fe built an adobe church, modeled after the old New Mexico mission architecture, especially to house this stone reredos. This new church is the largest mud building in the world and was purposely finished at the beginning of 1940 as a memorial of the 400th anniversary of the coming of Christianity to New Mexico, formerly New Spain. The Archbishop dedicated the new church to Christ the King and called it Cristo Rey. When the reredos was taken from its storage place, where the topmost panel was embedded in the adobe roof, it was discovered that on this hidden panel was carved Christ the King.

After officiating for three hours in the services on Good Friday, 1942, the pastor of Cristo Rey felt exhausted. But he had grieved much over the lack of faith in this present chaotic world, and his fatigue increased this worry; so he went back into the church to pray alone. When he looked up at the carved image of the Christ Child who is happily holding on His head a basket of grape vines and bread like a crown of heavenly joy, there on the keystone the priest no longer saw the Infant Christ. Instead the whole stone, as it were, had become an image of the grief-stricken face of the agonizing Christ, the Man of Sorrows crowned with thorns. Now that the transformation has once been seen, it can be discerned by all who view the carving.

Was the stone purposely carved to give the two aspects of Christ? Was it done so by some clever craftsman, or did God guide his hand unknown to himself? No confident answer can be given to these questions.

In the single belfry of Cristo Rey hang the bells from the ruins of some of the oldest Indian missions, those of Quarai, the "cities that died of fear" of Apache raids. These ancient bells of the newest New Mexico church, built of the earth itself in the oldest mission type, ring out from the loftiest city of the United States and its oldest capital city that Christ has atoned and that Christ is King.

Appendix

NEW MEXICO'S PUEBLO MISSIONS

"Pueblo" is the Spanish word for "village." The Pueblo Indians are, therefore, the Village Indians. There are eighteen pueblos left in New Mexico today, where the Indians are still living on parts of the four square leagues of land granted to each village by King Philip II of Spain. In the middle of each of these land grants, the King specified that a mission was to be built. The names by which these missions are known and a few facts about them are given below.

San Juan Mission: In the pueblo of San Juan de los Caballeros (St. John of the Gentlemen on Horseback). The mission is dedicated to San Juan Bautista (St. John the Baptist). This church was erected by Oñate's colonists in the pueblo then called Yunque, where the Spaniards first settled. It was probably completed in 1598. With the exception of the chapel of St. Augustine, Florida, it was the first place of worship built within the present confines of the United States. The mission was damaged in 1680 and repaired in 1698, although some writers insist that a new church was built after the reconquest. It was dismantled in 1890, and the church now in use at San Juan has always been a parish church.

Nambé Mission: San Francisco de Asis. The original mission was begun in 1598 and was the residential headquarters of several out-missions. The church with all its contents was destroyed in 1690, and a new church was built shortly after the reconquest in 1692. A few years ago attempts were made to restore the Nambé mission by adding a gabled roof. The corbels, vigas, altar railing, and practically all the wood of the structure have been used by Mr. and Mrs. Gerald Cassidy in their home on Canyon Road in Santa Fe.

Taos Mission: San Geronimo de Taos. This mission was built before 1617. It was burned in 1680. In 1695 a new church was erected, which continued in use until 1847. At this latter date the Taos Indians, incited by a group of Mexicans, rebelled against the United States and fortified themselves in the church. In the bombardment by the United States troops the church was wrecked and left in its present condition. The present church was erected later.

Jemez Mission: San Diego de Jemez. The first church was probably completed in 1599, but the first one of which there is positive record was erected in 1618 and dedicated to St. James (San Diego). This church is now in ruins. The exact date when the present church was built is not known; perhaps in the nineteenth century.

Ranchos de Taos

San Felipe Mission: San Felipe. In 1630 Benavides stated that the three Queres missions (San Felipe, Santa Ana, and Nuestra Senora de la Asuncion at Zia) had fine large churches and *conventos,* and that every Indian in the three pueblos had been baptized. The present church is a remodeling of the ruins of the original.

San Ildefonso Mission: San Ildefonso. This church was one of the most important of the early missions. It was destroyed in 1680. From 1692 to 1700 the *convento* was used for religious services. The present church was built in 1700, but has been remodeled out of all resemblance to its former self.

Picuris Mission: San Lorenzo de Picuris. Father Benavides in 1629 mentioned a fine mission at Picuris, serving a number of neighboring stations. The church was damaged in 1680 and was repaired immediately after the reconquest. It has since been repaired and remodeled at intervals so that little of the original structure remains.

Santa Ana Mission: Santa Ana de Alamillo. This church was built about 1600. Santa Ana was an outmission of the Asuncion at Zia before the rebellion; but after the reconquest, it was made a separate mission, the pueblo then being called Alamillo. The original church is still in use at Santa Ana.

Isleta Mission: San Augustin. The San Augustin mission must have been established before 1629; a church, a *convento* and an Indian school were there before Benavides wrote in 1629. The Spaniards here escaped the massacre of 1680, but the church and other mission buildings were destroyed. The present church was built after the Indians returned in 1692.

Santo Domingo Mission: Santo Domingo. This church was important enough in the early days of Spanish occupancy to have three padres, all of whom were killed on the first day of the rebellion. The church was not seriously damaged. It had been built in 1607 and was used until it fell into the Rio de Galisteo in 1886. The present church has been built since the latter date.

Cochiti Mission: San Buenaventura. This mission was probably founded about 1605. Cochiti was first an out-mission of Santo Domingo. The church was not destroyed in 1680, although the rest of the mission property was burned. It was repaired after the reoccupation and continues in service today.

Sandia Mission: Nuestra Senora de los Dolores. A mission dedicated to Our Lady of Sorrows was built in the Sandia pueblo at the beginning of the seventeenth century. This pueblo was abandoned between 1680 and 1692, and a new pueblo was built on another site. The first church and most of the old pueblo have disappeared. In the new pueblo a church dedicated to St. Francis was erected in 1714, followed by another in 1748, which is still standing, having been greatly remodeled.

Tesuque Mission: San Diego. A mission dedicated to St. Lawrence was established in the Tesuque pueblo before 1625. Attempts by the Indians to destroy it in 1680 resulted only in the woodwork being consumed, and in 1695 it was repaired and rededicated under the name of San Diego (St. James).

Pojuaque Mission: The name of the little mission church of Pojuaque is unknown, but its ruins still crown the brow of the hill. This hill is about 300 yards from the Taos road on the right side driving up from Santa Fe. Much of the old carved wood from this church has been used in the dining room at Boquet Ranch nearby.

Acoma Mission: San Estevan (Stephen) de Acoma. The first mission at Acoma was built in 1629. That church was remodeled or an entirely new church was built in 1699, which is still in use. All the material for the church, as well as the stone and earth for its artificial graveyard, 200 feet square, was carried up from the valley below on the backs of Indians.

Santa Clara Mission: Santa Clara de Asis. This mission was one of several founded by Father Benavides about 1629. It was destroyed in 1680, and the one built in 1696 is also in ruins. The present church was built after the "mission period."

Laguna Mission. The name given by the Spaniards is unknown. The original church, built in 1699, is still in use. It is dedicated to San José.

Cuarai, Abo, and Tabira Missions. There were six or seven missions in this Salinas region of New Mexico. Only the ruins of these three remain, and their real names are unknown. All were built between 1625 and 1630 under the leadership of Father Francisco Acevedo. These were the finest mission churches in all New Mexico and probably compared favorably with the best in other fields. They and their pueblos were abandoned about 1770 because of the hostility of Plains tribes, especially Apaches.

Zia Mission: Nuestra Senora de la Asuncion. A mission was established in the Zia pueblo at the same time as the one at Santa Ana and was dedicated to Our Lady of the Assumption. Both Zia and Santa Ana (Alamillo) were damaged by Spanish troops in 1687. The injured churches were later repaired and are still in use.

OTHER OLD CHURCHES

Near Santa Fe are several very old and interesting churches that were not missions. These were built for Spanish settlers.

Santa Cruz de Galisteo, in Santa Cruz, built in 1696; one of the largest in the state.

Ranchos de Taos church, built in 1772.

Fernandez de Taos, built in 1806.

Santuario in Chimayo, built in 1814.

San Felipe chapel in old Albuquerque, built in 1707.

In Santa Fe are the following:

Old San Francisco, built in 1714.

San Miguel, built between 1606 and 1626.

Rosario Chapel, built by De Vargas in 1693.

Nuestra Senora de Guadalupe, built about 1760.

DATES OF INDIAN DANCES

When the missions were built in the Indian pueblos, each village was given a patron saint. Often the village was afterward known by the name of this saint. Out of deference for the saint, the Indians placed their most important ceremony for that time of the year upon that day. Each year they celebrate the annual *fiesta* upon the day of the patron saint.

As far as we outsiders know, the only Indian ceremonials which can be definitely dated ahead from year to year are those occurring upon the saints' days.

Other ceremonies occur in certain months of the year, but the date is variable, depending upon the weather, the phases of the moon, the need of rain, and other natural or internal clan features.

Among the definitely dated ceremonies are the following:

January 6 (the Three Kings), celebrated in most of the pueblos with dances, usually animal dances. At San Ildefonso they invariably have the eagle dance; at Tesuque usually a buffalo dance; at Taos a deer dance; at Santa Clara often two dances.

January 23 (St. Ildefonse), a dance at San Ildefonso,

which may be a corn dance, a Comanche dance, a peace dance, or one that for some reason they call the French dance.

May 1 (St. Philip), corn dance at San Felipe.

June 13 (Our Lady of Sorrows), Sandia has a dance in which there are now few inhabitants to take part.

June 24 (St. John), at San Juan de los Cabelleros, its saint's day dance or sometimes two dances.

July 14 (St. Bonaventure), celebrated by Cochiti, generally with a corn dance, which frequently is accompanied by a downpour of rain.

July 26 (St. Anne), the day for the celebration at Santa Ana.

August 4 (St. Dominic), the great corn pageant at Santo Domingo.

August 10 (St. Lawrence), celebration at Picuris.

August 12 (St. Clare), the saint's day of Santa Clara pueblo. Until lately they have always had the "rain races," which last only about an hour. Recently, however, they have had other dances, such as the mountain-goat dance or the deer and antelope dance.

August 15 (Assumption), the date for Tsia's (Zia's) celebration.

August 28 (St. Augustine), the Isleta date.

September 2 (St. Stephen), the saint's day of Acoma.

September 19, substituted by the Laguna villages for celebration instead of their regular saint's day, which is March 19, St. Joseph's feast day.

September 30 (St. Jerome), the Taos *fiesta*. On the eve, at sunset, the Indians have an aspen-bough dance which lasts about half an hour. On the morning of the saint's day they have "rain races," and in the afternoon the clowns climb a slippery pole and perform other antics.

October 4 (St. Francis), celebrated by Nambé, usually with a deer dance. On the eve there is also a procession between bonfires in Santa Fe, by the Spanish-Americans. St. Francis is also the patron saint of Santa Fe.

November 12 (St. James), celebrated in Jemez and in Tesuque.

December 24, 25, 26, and 27, celebrated with dances at San Felipe, Santo Domingo, Jemez, Cochiti, San Juan, and others. Near midnight on Christmas Eve at San Juan they dance *los matachines* in the church; at San Felipe they have buffalo and deer dances in the mission; and the young people and children at Santo Domingo also dance in the church. These dances usually follow or precede a midnight Mass. On the 25th, *los matachines* is danced all day at San Juan and Cochiti. On the 26th, the San Juaneños have their *tortugas* (turtle) dance.

OTHER CELEBRATIONS

In January the Zunis have their sword-swallowing dance.

In February at San Juan they celebrate the seed-ball game, a shinny ball game played with a buckskin ball filled with seeds, which is knocked about until it bursts upon someone's field. The seeds are allowed to lie wherever they fall and sprout there to bring good luck to the owner of the field.

In February there are many secret kiva ceremonies.

Every alternate year in June or July the San Ildefonso people have an Ah-Van-yoh ceremony. The Ah-Van-yoh is the plumed or horned serpent that is the patron of rain and water.

November 1 (All Saints) is usually celebrated in Santo Domingo and elsewhere. In Santa Fe on the eve there is sometimes a procession.

During November at Santo Domingo takes place a "happiness dance," with gifts ranging from dead field mice (a great delicacy) through the gamut of canned goods to live chickens and rabbits.

In February the Santo Domingo Indians have a pageant of the coming of the "pink skins."

December 12 (Our Lady of Guadalupe) is celebrated with a *function* in many of the Spanish-American villages, such as Cordova.

In many of the pueblos Easter is generally celebrated with a group of dances.